Sexual
Orientation
in the
Workplace

Sexual Orientation in the Workplace

Gay Men, Lesbians, Bisexuals, and Heterosexuals Working Together

Amy J. Zuckerman and George F. Simons

SAGE Publications
International Educational and Professional Publisher
Thousand Oaks   London   New Delhi

For information, address:

SAGE Publications, Inc.
2455 Teller Road
Thousand Oaks, CA 91320
e-mail: order@sagepub.com

SAGE Publications Ltd.
6 Bonhill Street
London EC2A 4PU
United Kingdom

SAGE Publications India Pvt. Ltd.
M-32 Market
Greater Kailash I
New Delhi 100 048 India

Printed in the United States of America

Library of Congress Cataloging-in-Publication Data

Zuckerman, Amy J. (Amy Jo Allyn), 1967-
    Sexual orientation in the workplace: gay men, lesbians,
bisexuals, and heterosexuals working together / Amy J. Zuckerman,
George Simons.
        p.   cm.
    Includes bibliographic references.
    ISBN 0-7619-0119-1 (pbk.: alk. paper)
    1. Sexual orientation.   2. Personnel management.   3. Diversity in
the workplace.   I. Simons, George F.   II. Title.
HF5549.5.S45Z83   1995
658.3′045—dc20

96 97 98 99   10 9 8 7 6 5 4 3 2 1

Cover design: Robin Chew
Sage Managing Editor: Claudia A. Hoffman
Sage Copy Editor: Linda Gray

CONTENTS

PREFACE

This book consists of three main parts and a Resource Guide. First, we look at who makes up today's workforce with regard to sexual orientation and examine the facts about lesbians, gays, bisexuals, and heterosexuals. Second, we provide simple tools and exercises to address the personal dimensions of working realistically and effectively with diverse colleagues. Third, realizing that organizational culture is the context of our success and satisfaction on the job, we explore how leaders, groups, and organizations can set a positive climate and establish policies that support us all. The last section is a comprehensive listing of books, articles, videotapes, films, and sources of more information on this topic.

If you are a manager or supervisor, you already know that no company can afford to waste the talents and energy of any of its employees, whatever their sexual orientation. Unlike race, nationality, gender, and disabilities, there are fewer laws about sexual orientation to guide managers. Yet sexual orientation is one of the most controversial workforce topics today. Lesbian, gay, bisexual, and straight people need to find ways to work together creatively, productively, and without bias to minimize conflicts and job turnover.

If you are an employee, you may have experienced personally or through friends and coworkers the pain, fear, or prejudice that make sexual orientation one of the most challenging dimensions of diversity. Work has enough stresses of its own. When fears and misunderstandings about our coworkers disrupt our work, it is hard to find the creativity, joy, and satisfaction we deserve from our efforts.

Many organizations have already taken steps to provide a positive environment for workers of every sexual orientation. Tips and suggestions from them will help you do your job better.

This book does not ask people to change who they are, but it does ask them to do their part to create smoothly working relationships with others. Toward this end, it provides accurate information, stimulating exercises for self-discovery and mutual understanding, topics to discuss, and steps to take to improve your experience of working together.

So, welcome aboard, everyone. Sharpen your pencils and let's begin. By learning to understand, respect, and appreciate each other, we have everything to gain, working together.

—*Amy J. Zuckerman*

—*George F. Simons*

ABOUT THIS BOOK

Sexual Orientation in the Workplace is a book for both learning and doing. It is self-paced, has clear directions, and will involve you personally. Designed to be read with a pencil in hand, it is full of the kinds of exercises, examples, tips, and case studies that will help you see real-life implications.

You may want to use this book for *individual study.* For many people, sexual orientation is very hard to talk about. If that's you, this book's no-nonsense, practical approach is just what you need to begin to explore new information, sort out your feelings, and become comfortable enough to discuss the issues further. Perhaps you simply don't have the time or the opportunity to learn with others; if so, this book and a pencil are all that you need to get started.

Informal groups and support groups of individuals at work or in the community will discover that this book can serve as a rich source of topics for off-line discussion and study. It is perfect for a series of brown-bag luncheon themes and can provide a first resource for task forces and working teams.

Sexual Orientation in the Workplace is also designed to be used effectively as a text or workbook for *workplace training programs and public seminars* or as a supplement to work done in such formal programs. The structure provides a good curriculum for a short program, and many of the sections of this book are ready-made exercises for large- or small-group activities. The book can also be given as prework to persons about to attend a seminar or meeting that will deal with the issues of sexual orientation.

For organizations with individuals whose geographical locations or schedules make it difficult for them to come together for seminars and meetings, this book can be sent as a form of *remote location or off-hours training.*

Sexual Orientation in the Workplace is full of possibilities. One thing's for sure: Whatever your beliefs or sexual orientation, you will come away with a wealth of new understanding and ideas that you can use to make your working together with others a richer and more satisfying experience.

ACKNOWLEDGMENTS

Both of us are grateful to the many friends and coworkers in the field of diversity who have supported our efforts in putting this publication together. First thanks go to our colleague Nanci Luna Jiménez, the goddess of useful criticism. The position of Nanci's desk made her a day-by-day party to the goings-on that produced this book. Grateful thanks also go to Malati Shinazy, senior consultant at George Simons International.

A special round of thanks goes to those who read and commented on the earlier drafts of the book and from whose insights you will benefit in using it.

Bob Abramms, ODT, Inc.

Connie Bates, MULTUS, Inc.

Craig Gibson, The U.S. General Services Administration

Martha Legare, Legare Associates

Sharon Simma Lieberman, Lieberman & Associates

Ruth Poe, Human Resources Manager, Bay Federal Credit Union

Rita Risser, Fair Measures

Patti Roberts, Attorney at Law

Charles Seltzer, Building Bridges

Janet Stone, Consultant

Barbara Walker, Diversity Trainer, Educator and Consultant

Bradley Wilkinson, University of Atlanta

Rita Wuebbeler, Interglobe Cross-Cultural Business Services

We are also thankful to the many service organizations and agencies addressing sexual orientation issues who generously provided information and counsel when we needed it. We have chosen to list them in the Resources section of the book, where their names will be more useful to the reader. Special applause goes to Marquita Flemming, our editor at Sage Publications, whose excitement and dedication to this project has speedily brought it to an eager public.

The authors and the publisher of this book have used their best efforts in its preparation and make no warranty of any kind, expressed or implied, with regard to the instructions and suggestions contained here.

PART 1

Today's Diverse Workforce

Gay, lesbian, bisexual, and heterosexual people have been working together successfully since the beginning of time. What is different today is that many people now openly live out their sexual orientation. This challenges straight and gay people alike to deal with their fears and prejudices on the job so that all can be creative and productive together. In Part 1, we will look at today's diverse workplace, the setting in which this challenge takes place.

WORKPLACE REALITIES

Because sexual orientation is a topic that stirs debate, it is important at the outset to look at what we know with certainty about the issues. Here is a collection of basic facts that should underlie any discussion. Read them over carefully, then note your observations and questions on the page following this list.

1. Population

   If you are in an organization of any size, statistically speaking at least 3% to 12% of the people in your organization are gay, lesbian, or bisexual. This is a conservative estimate because various studies of sexual orientation use different definitions. Sometimes they go by how people define themselves. These percentages tend to be lower. Studies that measure sexual experience, on the other hand, point out that up to half of the population has at some point in life participated in sexual activity with a same-sex partner.

2. Distribution

   Homosexuality and bisexuality are distributed across the population. That means that women and men of every background, race, ethnicity, religion, class, and so on are homosexual and bisexual in roughly the same proportions. Gays, lesbians, and bisexuals exist in every country and virtually every culture around the world—and always have.

3. Identification

   Although certain identifiable trends, fashions, styles, and modes of expression exist in every culture, there is no valid set of criteria by which one can be certain that a person is straight, gay, lesbian, or bisexual. What people say they are is what we should always take as the most important indicator of their sexual orientation and how they want to be seen by others.

4. Responsibility

   Addressing sexual orientation issues is both a personal and an organizational responsibility. The feelings and fears of individuals tend to work their way into company policy. Company policy, in turn, tends to form the attitudes and behaviors of individuals. Using this cycle to make your company user-friendly for everybody requires a combination of personal effort and changes in organizational policy and culture.

5. Legal Protection

Unlike other targeted groups, gay, lesbian, and bisexual people are not currently protected against discrimination in employment by federal law. Some states and municipalities have extended these basic rights to them.

DIGESTING THE FACTS

1. Do any of the statements on the previous pages surprise you? If so, how?

_____

_____

2. How do they compare with the information you received growing up? What ideas about people's sexual orientation have you had to unlearn?

_____

_____

3. Are these facts common knowledge in your workplace, organization, or social circle? What kind of misinformation exists?

_____

_____

4. What are some of the most important things you would like to learn or questions you would like to answer by using this book? Here is a checklist of some possible outcomes. Add any that you feel are true for you.

       ✓
- ❑ It could help me better understand or accept a coworker or friend who is different from me.

- ❑ I want to be a better manager or supervisor of all my people.

- ❑ Why is sexual orientation important at work?

- ❑ If I'm better informed and comfortable with this, I could help others be, too.

- ❑ I have strong feelings about sexual orientation that I would like to sort out.

- ❑ I would like to help others understand me better.

- ❑ Others _____

_____

FINDING THE RIGHT WORDS

Many terms used today to talk about sexual orientation fall short of accurately and fairly describing both people and facts. The first step in discussing this topic is getting the words right. After all, we don't want to offend each other when we are learning how to work together smoothly.

On the next pages, you will find a list of words found in everyday speech with suggestions on how and when to use them so as not to offend in the workplace. Some words are in-group language used by gays, lesbians, and bisexuals but are not appropriate for straight people to use. In most cases, we would also discourage the use of these terms by anyone in the workplace because they may create divisions and add to confusion. Here are a few things to keep in mind:

1. One of the basic rules of diversity is that *people should have the right to choose the words that describe themselves or their group.* It is a good idea for outsiders to respect this choice. When talking to and about others, use the terms that the group or individual you are dealing with prefers. If you are unsure, ask. After all, other people are the experts on their own lives.

2. Second, remember that *the language about sexual orientation—like many other diversity topics—changes quickly* and will probably be in flux for the next few years. This list is a guide to usage current at the time of this writing. It is up to you to stay current with how language and society evolve on this topic.

3. Finally, remember that context and nonverbal signals make up a great part of communication. *How and when you say a word may be more important than the word you choose to use.*

Terms, Definitions, and Suggested Uses

Affectional Orientation

A lighter-sounding term sometimes used to mean **sexual orientation,** a term included in this list. *Appropriate.*

Affinity Groups

Groups that often start informally within an organization to address the needs of a specific population. In this context, we will be speaking largely about gay, lesbian, and bisexual groups, although the term is not limited to them— for example, there could be a Latino Managers group, a Women's Caucus, and so on in the same organization. *Appropriate.*

Bisexual

A person who is attracted to members of either sex. In long-term relationships with men or women, bisexuals may keep the bisexual label or call themselves gay, lesbian, or heterosexual as it applies. *Appropriate.*

Celibacy

The choice or circumstance of not participating in sexual activity. Gay people remain gay in sexual orientation even when they are celibate. This is no different from straight people who still consider themselves heterosexual when they are not sexually active with another person. People have their sexual orientation 24 hours a day. *Appropriate.*

Closet

A figure of speech used to describe the hiding of one's sexual identity—for example, "in the closet," "out of the closet," "closeted." *Appropriate.*

Coming Out

Telling yourself or other people about your gay, lesbian, or bisexual identity. *Appropriate.*

Domestic Partner

Also, simply *partner.* Anyone who lives with his or her lover. Domestic partner benefits, such as health care and retirement options, can be extended to live-in partners of gays, lesbians, and unmarried heterosexual couples. *Appropriate.*

Dyke

Derogatory toward lesbians and at the same time, in-group language for many lesbians. Of uncertain origin, although thought to come from Boadiccia, a woman warrior who allegedly had many female lovers. *Not appropriate for use by anyone in the workplace.*

Fag

Derogatory toward gay men. Leigh Rutledge, author of *The Gay Book of Lists,* suggests that fag comes from faggot, a bundle of wood used to light fires for burning people. *Faggot* came to mean the bodies of gay men when they were burned to death in the 14th century. Used as in-group language among some gays and lesbians. *Not appropriate for anyone to use in the workplace.*

Gay

The umbrella term for homosexual persons, although it most specifically refers to men who are attracted to and love men. It is equally acceptable and more accurate to refer to gay women as lesbians. *Appropriate, recommended.*

Gay Movement

The historical struggle to achieve dignity and equality for gays, lesbians, bisexual, and transgendered people. Not simply a political group, *gay movement* often includes the complete range of gay activism and visibility. *Appropriate.*

Heterosexual

People who are attracted to and love members of the opposite sex. *Appropriate.*

Heterosexism

The assumption that everyone is heterosexual. This belief and its accompanying behaviors communicate that people with heterosexual orientation are inherently better than those of other orientations. *Useful for technical discussion. Not appropriate when used as a label or accusation.*

Homophobia

Fear of homosexuality. *Useful for technical discussion. Not appropriate when used as a label or accusation. The adjective is* homophobic.

Homosexual

People who are attracted to members of the same sex. This is a term invented by psychiatrists around 1890 to describe what they saw as an illness. Most people today are choosing to use **gay** and **lesbian** instead. *Appropriate, not preferred.*

Internalized Homophobia

When gays, lesbians, and bisexuals believe the hurtful untruths about their group. Gay people sometimes act out this self-hatred against other gay men, lesbians, and bisexuals (e.g., in putting down a segment of the gay community) or against themselves (e.g., by abusing drugs or alcohol). *Useful for technical discussion.*

Lesbian

A woman who is attracted to and loves women. *Appropriate, recommended.*

Lover

One of the few terms gays and lesbians have to describe their romantic partners. Many seek a term that is less explicit, such as *life partner,* but to date none exists that really describes both the commitment and love in gay and lesbian relationships. *Appropriate.*

Outing

Announcing someone else's suspected or known sexual orientation to others without that person's consent. *Appropriate term, not an appropriate practice.*

Queer

There seems to be a split between generations about the acceptability of this term. Many younger gays, lesbians, and bisexuals feel that the term is refreshingly broad enough to include all parts of their identities and behavior. Many older gays and lesbians feel that the word has been hatefully used against them for too long and are reluctant to embrace it. *At this time, not appropriate for use by anyone in the workplace.*

Sexual Orientation

Our term of choice to describe everything that goes into why people are attracted to each other. Sexual orientation takes into account past experiences, current situations, and self-identification. This term is usually preferred to **sexual preference** because it conveys the fact that many people feel they are gay by nature, not simply by choice. *Appropriate, recommended.*

Sexual Preference

See **sexual orientation.**

Significant Other

A term created to signify the equivalent of spouse for people who live in loving partnership without marriage. This is one of the few terms gays and lesbians have to refer to lovers and partners. The term is also used by straight people to indicate an unmarried intimate partner in a committed relationship. *Appropriate.*

Straight

Common term used to mean a heterosexual person. Although some people of all sexual orientations take issue with the term, there is no better term in common use. For that reason, we have used both **straight** and **heterosexual** in this book. "Straight But Not Narrow" reads a popular T-shirt slogan that many heterosexual allies wear. *Appropriate. Be sensitive to those who might object.*

Transgendered

Men or women whose psychological self differs from the physical sex that they were assigned at birth. They feel more comfortable as a member of the other sex, or, not completely comfortable in either sex. *Transsexuals* have had medical procedures to alter their physical sexual characteristics, which is often called sex confirmation surgery. No one's sexual orientation can be altered by hormonal treatment or surgery. We have included transgendered people in this book because they experience types of prejudice similar to what gays, lesbians, and bisexuals experience. *Both terms are appropriate.*

Transvestite

A person who dresses in clothing of the other gender. This may or may not be connected with their sexual orientation. *Cross-dressing* is a common term for this behavior. *Both terms are appropriate.*

There are many vulgar terms that describe homosexual and heterosexual behavior that are obviously inappropriate and offensive to anyone. Occasionally in your discussion of the topic, you will have to let uninformed people know that such terms hurt you and others and should not be used.

ON SPEAKING TERMS

Questions for Research and Discussion

1. Now that you have at least skimmed over the list of words on the previous pages, what other terms come up when sexual orientation is discussed?

_____   _____

_____   _____

_____   _____

2. Circle the ones about which you have questions or concerns. Put a star next to the ones you think might offend someone.

3. How do people around you speak about sexual orientation or about people of different orientations when the topic is discussed? How do you think the people around you feel?

Socially?   _____

_____

At work?   _____

_____

4. How can we gently and good-heartedly remind each other when we use inappropriate terms by force of habit? What have you done in the past to change the words you use about other topics? How could you use that experience here?

_____

_____

_____

_____

NEW VIEWS ON OLD WORDS

In addition to finding words that do not offend, it's important to realize that one word may mean different things to different people. Words we use every day can mean something different in the context of gay men, lesbians, bisexuals, and their allies. It can seem that we are using completely separate dictionaries, depending on who we are.

EXERCISE

Use this list as a discussion starter with someone who is different from yourself. In the space at the right, note any differences that stand out for you while you talk together. If you don't have anyone you can have this discussion with, note your own answers, then read on to learn what these words sometimes mean for people in the gay community.

Being open

Family, immediate family

Parenting, coparenting

Pride

Relationships

Safety

NEW VIEWS

Here is a short "gay dictionary" for the words on the previous pages.

Being open

Although this can mean being relaxed and forthcoming about personal details, this can also mean coming out. Although by and large, gay men and lesbians believe that sexual behavior is a private matter, sexual identity or orientation is considered less so. The line of comfort varies from person to person and with each interaction.

Family, immediate family

Many gay, lesbian, and bisexual people have been rejected by their families of origin simply because they have a different sexual orientation. Many people create new families of supportive members that may include the following: intimate partners; children from previous marriages, adoption, or alternative insemination; and, quite commonly, ex-lovers and close friends. That feeling of kinship frequently extends to all other gay people, and two people who are strangers to one another may call each other family simply because they are both in the gay community.

Parenting, coparenting

Gays and lesbians are frequently labeled unfit parents by the U.S. court system. However, gays and lesbians can legally adopt children in some states, such as Massachusetts. *Coparenting* describes the role of the loving partner of the children's parent or guardian. Sometimes the partner can legally adopt the children.

Pride

Although some people think of pride as one of the seven deadly sins, to most gays, lesbians, and bisexuals, it simply means being happy with who you are. Gay pride celebrations are public expressions of this.

Relationships

Obviously, lesbian and gay intimate relationships look different from their heterosexual counterparts—both people are of the same sex! But, just as in straight relationships, some gay people are unattached and dating, while others have been in relationships for years. Although two men or two women may love each other for decades and may have their own commitment ceremonies, they cannot marry each other in most of the world. Courageously, these commitments continue without the support of a traditional religious or legal system. We need to respect that no two relationships are alike, including those of bisexuals and heterosexuals.

Safety

Safety is a big issue among gays, lesbians, and bisexuals because each interaction brings up how safe it is to come out. The danger of a violent antigay assault is often very real. In addition, encouraging safer sex or better protection from sexually transmitted diseases such as HIV, the virus that causes AIDS, has unquestionably become a priority among gays, lesbians, and bisexuals.

HOMOPHOBIA: COUNTING THE COSTS

Homophobia, the fear of gay people, causes both heterosexual and gay people to react in strange ways. Sometimes, it forces gay people into the "corporate closet"—that is, they go to great lengths to hide their sexual orientation at work. Homophobia separates people who could work together productively and enjoy each other's company. It may cause them to avoid each other or sabotage each other's efforts. In some cases, homophobia results in harassment, violence, or expensive litigation that can destroy the lives of the individuals involved and drain the organization's resources.

Here are examples of situations in which the costs are adding up. In the space beneath each example, list what you believe would be one personal cost to the people involved and one cost to the organization to which the individuals belong. When you have finished, compare your answers to those of the authors. Here is an example:

Sarah never talks about herself when the others are discussing their husbands and wives. She knows that they think she is cold and reserved, but she is afraid to tell them about her life with her woman partner for fear of being rejected or even fired.

Personal cost
There may be damaged relationships between coworkers; the job becomes uncomfortable for Sarah and those around her.

Organizational cost
Sarah always feels on guard; she may quit for a more comfortable job; the company must spend time and money to replace her.

Now you try it. What do you think the costs are in each of the following situations?

1. *When the other managers—all men—go to lunch, they have gradually stopped inviting Wilson, who is rumored to be gay.*

Personal cost _____

_____

Organizational cost _____

_____

2. *Mae Linn gives preferential treatment to gay men when hiring applicants. She believes that they are more creative and sensitive and will treat women better than straight men will.*

Personal cost _____

_____

Organizational cost _____

_____

3. *Since telling others that she is a lesbian, Jayne has noticed that David, a coworker, has begun to make passes at her. She has heard via the grapevine that he has told his buddies she will be a "real challenge."*

Personal cost _____

_____

Organizational cost _____

_____

4. *Stephen has felt depressed for several weeks and has given people around the office different explanations. When his coworkers discover that he and a long-term male lover just broke up, they wonder what else Stephen is hiding.*

Personal cost   _____

_____

Organizational cost   _____

_____

5. *Rosita has heard that several of the caregivers at the day care center where she leaves her children are gay. She is embarrassed to discuss the issue with her supervisor, Carmen. She simply tells Carmen that she can no longer work mornings.*

Personal cost   _____

_____

Organizational cost   _____

_____

6. *Angelo is afraid to tell his subordinates to get back to work and stop playing tricks on their gay coworker. He is afraid that his subordinates will think of him as soft or suspect that he is gay even though he is not.*

Personal cost   _____

_____

Organizational cost   _____

_____

7. *When some people where Thomas works find out that he is gay, his coworkers and even his manager make AIDS jokes in front of him.*

Personal cost   _____

_____

Organizational cost   _____

_____

8. *Judy, a lawyer and a lesbian, is the first to be laid off from her $55,000-a-year position when her firm faces downsizing. She feels she was first to be fired because of the senior partners' homophobia.*

Personal cost   _____

_____

Organizational cost   _____

_____

On the next page, we've listed some of our responses to these situations. Read them to see if they add to your understanding of the issues. Do you agree or disagree? Why?

Personal Cost	Organizational Cost
1. Wilson becomes an outcast. His colleagues fail to confront their prejudice. Lack of trust on both sides grows. Loss of profitable networking.	1. Loss of valuable perspectives, consensus, and team spirit among the group.
2. Individuals devalued, stereotyped, and set up to fail unrealistic expectations.	2. Wrong people may be hired. Mae Linn's bias will reveal itself, causing hurt, perhaps a claim.
3. Humiliation for both parties. Hostile work environment for Jayne.	3. Possibly an expensive harassment lawsuit. Dysfunction due to homophobia.
4. Gossip. Mistrust.	4. Strained working relationships.
5. Living in fear for her family and children. Loss of income or job. Damage to reputation for not seeming to value her work more highly.	5. Work loss. Her beliefs are seen as disruptive to work schedules. The company's tolerance of employee diversity decreases.
6. Loss of personal respect for all involved. Damage to Angelo's career as manager.	6. Breakdown of work discipline. Potential hostile-environment lawsuit.
7. Thomas is upset and considers quitting. He is upset because his coworkers joke about the tragedy of AIDS. They are uncomfortable with his sexuality.	7. Company could get reputation as hostile toward gays and lesbians. Cost of replacing Thomas. If the firm tracks or fires people it suspects are HIV-positive, it could be sued.
8. Loss of professional standing, money, and time job searching.	8. Judy may sue if her firing was discriminatory.

OUR ORGANIZATION'S CLIMATE

Where do your organization and the people in it tend to stand on issues of sexual orientation? Are they warm and receptive to employee differences or cold and forbidding? Find the statements to the right of the centigrade thermometer that are true of your organization. When you find an item that is true of where you work, write in the temperature in the blank immediately to the left of the thermometer. Then turn to the next page to calculate your organization's temperature.

Warm and Receptive

_____60°   Programs on sexual orientation are a normal part of diversity training.

_____50°   We offer health and other benefits to nonmarried, live-in partners of employees, regardless of sexual orientation.

_____40°   Partners of gays, lesbians, bisexuals, and straight people are always recognized on company invitations and so on.

_____30°   The concerns and needs of gay, lesbian, and bisexual employees are being heard by management through affinity groups, allies, liaisons, and so on.

_____20°   Employees were told that antigay discrimination will be punished.

_____10°   Gays, lesbians, and bisexuals have started an unofficial employee group.

0° FREEZING POINT

_____-10°   Gay people might be tolerated on the surface, but they are excluded from informal networking.

_____-20°   One or two people are known to be gay, but no one talks about it.

_____-30°   Everyone is afraid to talk about sexual orientation for fear of what people might think about them.

_____-40°   People often tell antigay and AIDS jokes.

_____-50°   Persons who came out as gay, lesbian, or bisexual have been shunned, harassed, fired, or physically injured.

Cold and Forbidding

WHAT'S THE TEMPERATURE?

To read the temperature of your organization, total the degrees above freezing and subtract the total of degrees below freezing. Below, state reasons for making the choices you did.

Degrees above freezing: _____

Degrees below freezing: _____

Our organizational temperature: _____

What kinds of things happen at work that made you answer as you did? Try to give one example of workplace policy or behavior for each mark on the thermometer that you made.

_____

_____

_____

_____

_____

_____

_____

_____

SETTING A NEW CLIMATE

If your organization improved its climate for everyone concerning the issues of sexual orientation, on whose desk would the assignment fall? Whose job is it to make sure everyone in the organization is appreciated and works well together? Is it management's? The personnel department's? Is it your responsibility, no matter what your position? Answer the following questions:

Who is responsible, who could make a difference: you, a line manager, personnel director, a CEO? Fill in the blanks with one of those four choices.

1. A new gay employee in your generally tough workplace is left to test the waters of tolerance alone.

   _____

2. A proactive stance is needed to educate all employees before any gay or lesbian is known to be on staff.

   _____

3. The few gay, lesbian, and bisexual people at work need assertive behavior from supportive coworkers when people say offensive things.

   _____

4. All workers need to know that shunning, harassing, or discrimination of any kind will not be tolerated.

   _____

ON THE NEXT PAGES

We next examine how an organization reaches the goal of welcoming all employees so that it can truly attract—and select from—the best and the brightest. On the following pages are some questions about who takes responsibility in your organization and real-life case studies from firms showing how they have effectively handled sexual orientation. Read each case study and answer the questions that follow.

THE VIEW FROM THE TOP

Case Study #1

Borland International
Scotts Valley, California

At this Silicon Valley firm, the employees' desire for change inspired president, chairman, and CEO Philippe Khan to make powerful policy changes to ensure the fair treatment of all workers. A policy barring discrimination on the basis of sexual orientation was put into effect in 1992. Partners of gays, lesbians, bisexuals, and unmarried heterosexuals now receive health benefits. In addition, CEO Khan has become an activist on the topic, volunteering to testify before Congress in support of the Employment Non-Discrimination Act of 1994 regarding fair treatment of gays, lesbians, and bisexuals in the workplace.

Your Turn

What tone has the head of your organization set for the rest of the employees on the issue of employees' sexual orientation? Has there been silence? Do you know of resistance from top management to others' efforts to provide diversity training, domestic partner benefits, or an affinity group for gay, lesbian, and bisexual employees? Or has your leadership truly been fearless in dealing head-on with this issue?

Below, give your perspective on what leadership has done to deal with different sexual orientations of employees. Or simply think about how his, her, or their actions have set the tone for the organization on sexual orientation.

_____

_____

_____

_____

ON A PERSONNEL NOTE

Case Study #2

Genentech, Inc.,
South San Francisco, California

Lisa Kenney in the Medical Affairs Division at this biotechnology company credits the diversity manager in the Human Resources (HR) Department with being a vital link between gay, lesbian, and bisexual employees and the top management. The employee group opened a dialogue with HR, which had already added a nondiscrimination clause regarding sexual orientation to its policies. HR brought the issue to former CEO G. Kirk Raab, who became their advocate. "It was just a matter of getting him the information," says Kenney.

With Raab's approval, HR started a diversity initiative inclusive of sexual orientation issues and instituted a domestic partner benefits plan. Upper management now actively seeks feedback from gay, lesbian, and bisexual employees on both employee and Genentech issues.

The company has gone on to support the AIDS Walk fundraiser and displays sections from the AIDS memorial quilt at the site. Moreover, Kenney says gay, lesbian, and bisexual employees have improved the quality of the company's products by sharing their perspectives as gay people. They contribute valuable information on the gay community's product usage, such as for an AIDS drug under development.

Your Turn

Sometimes the human resources or personnel department can play a crucial part in setting the organization's tone by both responding to employees who want changes and accurately and fairly relaying concerns to top management.

What do you see as the role for your personnel or human resources department in establishing policy and educating people about sexual orientation?

_____

_____

What is their next step in accomplishing these goals?

_____

_____

THE EMPOWERED EMPLOYEE

Case Study #3

AT&T,
Denver, Colorado

The gay, lesbian, and bisexual network at AT&T is testimony to the possibilities of the empowered employee. Technical Manager Margaret Burd is the national cochair of LEAGUE, the AT&T gay, lesbian, and bisexual employee group. The 1,500 to 2,000 members of LEAGUE, which started in 1987, are in nearly 30 locations and have been a network nationally since 1992. The group has a national assembly, officers, standing committees, and a yearly meeting held the day before an annual corporate development conference.

To get sexual orientation included in diversity training, Burd's on-site group formed and began communicating with upper management in Denver through a consultant. The idea took off, said Burd. "People stopped by each other's offices, saying, 'There's this new group that spans the company.' " In preparation for their first conference, they also began to work with similar employee groups in New Jersey, Orlando, Atlanta, and other locations. At that point, the national LEAGUE "sprang up," according to Burd.

Now LEAGUE members communicate with each other via electronic mail and, of course, the telephone. They have strong allies in top management and boast a comprehensive corporate diversity board. LEAGUE's current work includes pushing for domestic partner benefits, providing education for LEAGUE members and the rest of the corporation, and helping with AT&T's marketing toward gay and lesbian customers.

Your Turn

In some organizations, employees are encouraged to help set the tone for everyone. According to this management philosophy, empowering employees to shape the organization will result in more productivity and, ultimately, better business. In other workplaces, corporate culture does not allow for employee involvement.

How are you, as an employee, able to affect your organization regarding diversity? Do you know what the limits are?

_____

_____

_____

_____

Considering the possible risks and rewards involved, what are you willing and able to do to be active on this topic?

_____

_____

_____

_____

PART 2

The Personal Challenge

We each face the challenge of working on our own beliefs and behaviors around others' sexual orientation. Part 2 will look at our own patterns of thought and how we can overcome damaging stereotypes about each other. With this information, we can increase our understanding of, respect for, and cooperation with those whose sexual orientation and experience of life may be quite different from our own.

JOB STEREOTYPES

In the United States, we tend to define ourselves by the jobs we hold or the work we perform. "What do you do?" is often the first question we ask after meeting someone new. How do people's ideas about certain jobs stereotype the people who fill those jobs?

Here are some ways in which individuals have felt unfairly stereotyped because of their jobs. Notice that both positive and negative stereotypes can create misunderstandings that affect our success on the job.

— Jon (straight male hairdresser): *I get tired of people thinking I am gay simply because I'm a hairdresser. So I deal creatively and sensitively with my largely female clientele—that's just good business.*

— Jefferson (gay military police, retired): *For a long time nobody believed I was gay even when I told them point blank.*

— Rupert (straight clergyman): *Just because I am a priest, it is no indication that I am gay or a child molester. Such innuendo is hurtful both to people with my calling and to men who really are gay.*

— Nanci (straight flight attendant): *People sometimes think I'm a lesbian because I'm bigger than most women I work with and I keep my hair short. I also don't think I need to wear a lot of makeup. Why do people think sexual orientation depends on your size and little things about your appearance?*

— Vlad (heterosexual beat cop): *I feel a lot of pressure to be rough and tough, especially on gay people.*

Gays and lesbians get caught in coworkers' stereotypes concerning sexual orientation.

— Ruth (lesbian human resources director): *I'm a woman whose lesbian identity is known by everyone at work. But I know one of the major reasons I can succeed in my job is because I dress and look the part of a "feminine" woman. If I fit a stereotype of a "butch" lesbian, I'd never make it.*

— Kurumi (lesbian plumber): *Because I am a lesbian, my male peers think I am more capable at my work than my straight women coworkers. They see me as "one of the boys." Also, with me they feel they don't have to worry about sexual attraction or involvement.*

— Angie (lesbian marketing executive): *Because they know I am a lesbian, my male colleagues feel more competitive with me in intense working situations than they do with some of my straight female peers. I feel they go out of their way to sabotage my projects.*

— Santiago (gay medical doctor): *I am in a monogamous relationship, have tested negative for HIV, and use thorough precautions in my work. However, my clientele is dwindling because people fear I might infect them with AIDS.*

1. How have you been stereotyped by others as a result of your present job or one you held in the past? What was the job? What was the stereotype? How did you feel?

_____

_____

_____

_____

2. What were the costs to you of being stereotyped? What could or couldn't you do as a result? How did being stereotyped help or hinder your performance or success on the job?

_____

_____

_____

_____

3. Positive stereotypes may have short-term benefits, but they usually have long-term or large-scale costs. For Kurumi, the lesbian plumber whose words we read on the previous page, it may be easier to work with these men on a day-to-day basis, but in the long run, tensions with other employees resulting from her treatment can be damaging. If the stereotype of you was positive, what might have been some of the less desirable consequences?

_____

_____

_____

_____

MYTHS VERSUS FACTS

Most workplace stereotypes cause discomfort and irritation. The most destructive stereotypes about sexual orientation have become myths of huge proportions and give rise to very dangerous fears. Here are some of these myths set side by side with facts. Please see the book list in Part 4 for plenty of sources to explode these and other myths.

Myth	Fact
The only "real" men and women are heterosexual.	Studies of human sexuality as early as the Kinsey Report (1948)[1] consistently show that human sexual behavior is on a continuum. Kinsey found that 46% of people studied fell somewhere between exclusively heterosexual and exclusively homosexual.
Bisexuals have not grown up yet, are in a phase, or are flaky, indecisive individuals.	In the United States, 20 million people call themselves bisexual. Their range of emotional and psychological maturity is similar to that of the general population.
Gays and lesbians are sexual predators always on the prowl for innocent children.	In proportion to their percentage of the general population, heterosexuals perform far more child sexual abuse than do gay people.
AIDS is a disease of gay men.	The World Health Organization says 75% of people with AIDS were infected through heterosexual sex. In the United States, heterosexual teens are the largest growing segment of the population with AIDS.
Gay, lesbian, or bisexual individuals are bad for an organization's morale.	Of Fortune 1000 companies in a 1993 survey, 72% felt that a nondiscrimination policy would improve morale and productivity.[2]
Good straight sex would cure most lesbians.	Being lesbian is normal for a percentage of the population. There is nothing to cure.

Can you add to the list?

_____   _____

_____   _____

Confronting stereotypes with facts is rarely enough to help people shed the deep emotional fears and suspicions that they have grown up with. Because we usually got this misinformation through emotional channels, it is often embedded in such a way that unemotional facts cannot easily dislodge it. Person-to-person connections go far in illuminating and eliminating stereotypes.

HOW WE ACT AROUND EACH OTHER

Everyone has unanswered questions about what to do and what not to do when it comes to sexual orientation. Here are some of them. Check the statements you would like to answer for yourself or discuss with others.

✓

❑ 1. What do I do with my discomfort with a coworker who suddenly tells me he is gay? How should I act? I don't feel I can put my hand on his shoulder the way I used to do. He might think I'm making a pass at him.

❑ 2. How can I get people to accept my partner? After eight years, I still have to refer to my lover as "my roommate," and I don't bring her to the annual picnic.

❑ 3. I am a lesbian who is pregnant. I'm constantly asked about the baby's father and my marital status. Why does it matter, especially here at work?

❑ 4. How do I deal with my feelings and those of my straight (I think) male coworkers about gay men? Many of us straight men are uncomfortable around gay men. Why else would there be all this posturing to appear macho? Why else do we have the nervous laughter and the put-down jokes?

❑ 5. Why is it still acceptable to beat up gay people verbally or even physically? How do we stop the snide remarks, jokes, and hostile tactics?

❑ 6. I am an openly gay man who's tired of being set up with straight women. First my mother did it; now my colleagues at work try to "fix" me. I want to be accepted for who I am.

❑ 7. How do I know who's gay or straight? You just can't see gay people like you see other groups at the office. They're white, black, Asian, Latino, all races, all kinds. Some are very "masculine" or "feminine" in a traditional sense. Others reflect a specific gay culture in their dress and behavior. Do I need to know?

❑ 8. As a traditionally religious person with strong family values, how do I reconcile the demands for tolerating differences with my faith and my responsibility to hand my religious teachings on to my children?

❑ 9. There must be a "glass ceiling" for my openly gay coworkers. Whatever their talent and dedication, they don't get the promotions they deserve.

❑10. Several of my friends have AIDS. I wish I could do more to ease the pain that being social outcasts causes them.

There is no single perfect answer to these questions. Confronting stereotypes by getting to know each other as real individuals and speaking directly and fearlessly will make it safe for us to share our differences and be respected. Who will you talk to today?

GENDER BENDING

Differences in sexual orientation allow us to look more closely at how our culture defines masculinity and femininity. Gay men are frequently stereotyped as more effeminate, and lesbians are stereotyped as more masculine. Straight and gay people alike encounter situations in which they are seen as not "female" or "male" enough.

But some lesbians appear more traditionally feminine than many straight women, and many gay men seem more masculine than many straight men. Also, straight people can be labeled as gay just because they fit part of a stereotype of a gay person—based on dress, appearance, profession, behavior, voice, hobbies, and tastes.

Remember that we cannot be held responsible for the incorrect information we got when we were young about different kinds of people. We are responsible for what we do with that information now and whenever it pops into our minds.

When we look at someone, our minds try to interpret him or her. We pick up clues that trigger information from our cultural background about how to treat that person. When the signals we receive are not clear according to our cultural norms, *we* get confused. We wonder why a man has earrings or why a woman prefers men's suits and short hair. We may ask ourselves, "Why don't they look like *I think* they are supposed to?"

Sometimes people respond to their own confusion by attacking others out of fear and anger. They may lash out at the person who doesn't fit their notions. Many, many gays and lesbians are survivors of brutal attacks because they *represented* a threat to another person's beliefs. Many gays and lesbians have been killed in this country for that reason.

Describe one way your notion of men has changed since you were young.

_____

_____

_____

Now describe one way your notion of women has changed since then.

_____

_____

_____

Narrow definitions of gender limit us all. Straight and gay people alike encounter situations in which they are seen as not female or male enough. Fortunately, in recent years, increased informality and other changes in society have broadened people's definitions. When we stop using the stereotypes of gays and lesbians on everyone, we are free to see all people as simply who they are, not who we think they should be.

GAY AND LESBIAN IDENTITY
The Work Closet

Most of us grew up with "a skeleton in the closet," a story that was never talked about in our families. Gays, lesbians, and bisexuals are all too familiar with *The Closet*. It's a personal closet, the place where, when they believe they must, gay people hide everything having to do with sexual orientation: gay friends, lovers, long-term partners, community activities, and pride in who they are. Heterosexuals experience the closet when it is not safe for them to talk about gay, lesbian, and bisexual relatives and friends.

Millions of gay men, lesbians, and bisexuals are hiding in their closets right now at work. They are afraid of being ostracized, harassed, and fired from their jobs. In a perfect world, where no one needed secrecy for protection, thousands of gays and lesbians would be open about those they love and live with and the myriad of personal details that straight people never think twice about sharing with coworkers. But fear keeps the closet door firmly shut.

Many have carefully weighed the options: "Should I keep up the energy-draining but profitable charade by staying 'straight' at work, or should I bring both sides of my life together in total honesty, whatever it costs?" Millions have opened their closet doors and been accepted by their coworkers. Others do not feel that level of comfort. Whatever the decision made, it is the right choice for that person and his or her work environment. We each can make the best assessment of our own situations.

What's in Your Closet?

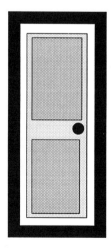

All of us, straight or gay, have things we don't reveal at work. Sometimes they are events out of the past or they are events too personal, delicate, or risky to mention. Think for a moment about some of the things you would rather not discuss with others at work.

Let the closet door be a reminder to you of how you protect yourself and others by silence. Also remember how important it is to respect others' privacy when they choose to remain silent.

COMING OUT

For gays, lesbians, and bisexuals, coming out may have several parts and phases. The first part is coming out to yourself, then to your family and friends, the people in your life. The part we will talk about here is coming out at work.

Although it is becoming more acceptable to be openly gay or lesbian, "coming out" is not easy, nor is it free of risk. Each gay man, lesbian woman, and bisexual person must have the right to control the timing. Social pressures lead even straight people to feel that everyone who is gay should come out. They might overestimate the climate of acceptance. No one, gay or straight, can or should make the decision for another. *Outing,* publicizing that another person is gay, is never acceptable in the workplace.

Gays and lesbians are different from visibly recognizable minorities because they must decide whether to come out whenever meeting someone new or every time a personal topic comes up at work. If they stay in the closet, they may cope by not telling the whole story or by simply avoiding personal conversations. This takes a lot of energy.

If you have a coworker who you think is in the closet or who was in the closet, take a moment to appreciate his or her coping skills. This person has good intuition and deserves your respect. Appreciate her or his willingness to come to work every day in spite of the extra stress involved.

The stress of not being open either to ourselves or to our coworkers is taxing. Gays, lesbians, bisexuals, and their heterosexual allies who deal every day with the silence and intolerance of their companies or organizations deserve a lot of affirming messages. They need to hear that they are not shameful and that even the smallest details of their lives that reflect their sexual orientation are worthy of having someone hear them.

Another Point of View

Some gay and lesbian people feel more comfortable not coming out about their sexual orientation in their work environment. They may not think it's an appropriate topic to discuss with coworkers and colleagues. They may be offended by insistence that they share this personal detail. Both gay and straight people should respect different points of view.

COMING OUT AT WORK

Coming out is the single most effective way for gays, lesbians, and bisexuals to show the reality of their lives and the diversity of the gay, lesbian, and bisexual community. By knowing a gay man, lesbian, or bisexual, a person suddenly puts a face on the abstract concept of homosexuality or bisexuality.

For those gay men, lesbians, and bisexuals who are currently in the process of coming out, we offer the following:

---

10 Tips for Coming Out

1. When you feel it is safe, talk openly about your life with those you know and love. Commit to doing this every day.

2. Consider coming out in your place of work.

3. Contact gay, lesbian, and bisexual organizations in your professional field.

4. Join a local and national gay and lesbian organization for information and support. Pass the name on to the Human Resources Department at your workplace.

5. If you are involved with someone of the same sex, include him or her in your professional events and occasions.

6. Join your firm's gay, lesbian, bisexual, and allies group, if there is one. If not, consider starting one.

7. Work to have your organization add sexual orientation to its nondiscrimination statement. Work to have domestic partner benefits established.

8. Support companies that support gays and lesbians.

9. Apply your experience, connections, and perspective as a lesbian, gay man, or bisexual person to your professional work.

10. Be true to yourself and simply be the person you have been all of your life.

SEXUAL ORIENTATION AT WORK

The Invisible Norm

Many people think sexual orientation should not be discussed at all in the workplace. What they don't realize, however, is that sexual orientation is *already* shaping the norms within organizations—it's simply that the accepted topic is *heterosexual orientation.* This is almost always invisible to the straight people because it seems so normal to them. Heterosexuals who are not married are frequently left out as well. The following are some examples:

- "I don't know why you're not married. You're good looking and you're on the 'up and up' around here."
  Because I'm gay! Please don't assume I'm straight just because I haven't said otherwise.

- "We offer benefits for husbands and wives of employees, plus family leave in case of a death in either of your immediate families. You have to be legally married to your spouse."
  My lover's father is dying of cancer. Can't I get off work to be with Marjorie when he dies?

- "The company would pay for your husband to come too, if you are married."
  Will you pay for my partner, or is this offer just for married heterosexuals?

Heterosexuals are usually unconscious of how strongly heterosexuality is normally the requirement at work and how it is reinforced day after day: in the way people speak, by the photos of spouses and family where people work, by the jokes told in the lunchroom, by company invitations that exclusively address "employees and their *spouses."* Sometimes the norm is consciously articulated in companies by leaders who say they want only "family-oriented" employees. Gay people have families and are parts of families, too.

Remember to Be Human

From time to time, we enjoy stopping the flow of work for a short break to discuss the people in our lives and our activities. Opening these conversations to everyone is relatively easy if we remember that no one needs to stop being who they are to have meaningful exchanges with others.

A REVERSE QUESTIONNAIRE

by Dr. Mary Ann Tucker and Sharon Young

For many years, training workshops at Digital Equipment Corporation used this questionnaire. The items on it are very similar to questions commonly asked of lesbians and gay men, but the authors of the list have given them a twist by asking them of straight people. Whether you are gay or straight, read the questionnaire through and mull it over. What is your reaction?

1. What do you think caused your heterosexuality?

2. At what age did you decide you were heterosexual?

3. With all the problems heterosexuals face, would you want your child to be heterosexual?

4. Is it possible that heterosexuality is just a phase you may grow out of?

5. Is it possible your heterosexuality stems from a neurotic fear of others of the same sex?

6. If you've never slept with a person of the same sex, is it possible that all you need is a good same-sex lover?

7. To whom have you disclosed your heterosexual tendencies?

8. Why do heterosexuals feel compelled to seduce others into their lifestyle?

9. Why do you insist on flaunting your heterosexuality? Why can't you just be who you are and keep quiet about it?

10. A disproportionate majority of child molesters are heterosexual. Do you consider it safe to expose your children to heterosexual teachers?

11. With all the social support marriage receives, the divorce rate is still 50%. Why are there so few stable relationships among heterosexuals?

12. Why do heterosexuals place so much emphasis on sex?

13. Considering the menace of hunger and overpopulation, can the human race survive if everyone were heterosexual like yourself?

14. There seem to be very few happy heterosexuals. Techniques have been developed that might enable you to change. Have you considered therapy?

My Reaction

_____

_____

_____

INTERMISSION

Use this space to jot down personal thoughts or notes for discussion from the work you have done so far in this book. Perhaps include questions that remain unanswered for you about sexual orientation in your work environment. Note the things you want to think about and consider doing differently.

What I have learned so far:

_____

_____

_____

_____

Questions I still have:

_____

_____

_____

_____

What I would like to change:

_____

_____

_____

_____

RELIGION AND SEXUAL ORIENTATION

Despite—or perhaps even because of—the separation of church and state in constitutional law and public policy, religious values and their expression are very strong in North America today. This same policy has also contributed to the paradoxical situation in which people treat religion as a highly private affair or debate it with great passion. Sexual orientation has often been the subject of such debate, from legislatures to company cafeterias.

Within the conscience of the religious person, values of love, fairness, compassion, and caring for others may stand side by side with strong beliefs that homosexuality is wrong and dangerous to individuals and family life. Given this religious and cultural environment, it is not surprising that many gay, lesbian, and bisexual individuals have had to struggle with their own consciences and feelings to find peace and self-esteem within a religious tradition.

The history of culture and religion shows that homosexuals have been seen as everything from sinners of the worst sort—people to be condemned, cast out, or even executed—to sacred intermediaries with the gods—figures to be respected and revered.

How conflicting values become reconciled in religious groups and individuals is a larger issue than we can deal with fully in this book. However, we can provide some useful tips for handling this clash of values when it arises in the workplace. On the next page are some things you can do as a peer or as a manager if you find religious issues in strong conflict with efforts to improve the situation or policies concerning gays, lesbians, and bisexuals. These tips will serve you well in dealing with this issue outside work as well.

First, circle the number on the scale below each tip to indicate how well you think you are able to perform it. Then make a note about how you can improve.

1. *Calmly, respectfully let others know what you believe and stand for.* People may not accept what you say, but they have to deal with your real presence in their lives day after day. If you wear your values on your sleeve and are highly defensive about them, you invite attack. Your personal values, however, tend to be taken more seriously by others when they are seen as well integrated with the rest of your life.

Easy for me ⟵ 1 —— 2 —— 3 —— 4 —— 5 ⟶ Difficult for me

Improvement _____

_____

2. *Respect people's beliefs. Do not attempt to change them.* Decent, fair, and acceptable behavior toward all employees is important here. Someone who has believed all her or his life that homosexuality is wrong is not going to change her or his opinion overnight any more than someone who is gay, lesbian, or bisexual is going to change if told she or he is wrong. However, everyone in such conflicts must behave in accordance with public laws and company nondiscrimination policies.

Easy for me ⟵ 1 —— 2 —— 3 —— 4 —— 5 ⟶ Difficult for me

Improvement _____

_____

3. *Call on your own and others' values of tolerance, compassion, kindness, and so on.* Respect for such values is usually found in some form in religious and spiritual belief systems. You can appeal to these values to override fear and prejudice.

Easy for me ⟵ 1 —— 2 —— 3 —— 4 —— 5 ⟶ Difficult for me

Improvement _____

_____

4. *Listen to people, not their slogans.* Sometimes, religious slogans mask other issues that people are afraid of or don't know how to talk about. Attacking what they say as bigotry or bias simply hardens their position. Listening to their worries and concerns and accepting these as real, on the other hand, will go a long way toward softening resistance and finding common ground.

Easy for me ⟵ 1 —— 2 —— 3 —— 4 —— 5 ⟶ Difficult for me

Improvement _____

5. *Show by example the attitudes and actions that you want to see from others.* Modeling day by day what you believe in and demonstrating the social and peer norms you would like to create in your workplace are usually much more effective than trying to talk people out of their beliefs.

Easy for me ⟵ 1 —— 2 —— 3 —— 4 —— 5 ⟶ Difficult for me

Improvement _____

USE YOUR RELIGIOUS RESOURCES

Here are a few more suggestions that can help you personally and professionally deal directly with issues of sexual orientation and religion. Each suggestion has some work space after it to help you think about it.

✓ *Know your own faith and beliefs and learn about those of others.* Frequently, people are confused about their own religion's stand on sexual orientation issues, and religious groups themselves can be divided on the topic. This is part of the natural growth process of a religious group: Traditions and values must be constantly renewed and applied to what people face in a changing world. This is never a simple matter but always an important debate as people sincerely try to understand how their faith should be lived out right now.

For example, in 1992, a wide range of Jewish and Christian religious leaders were asked to give their personal opinions about the questions below.[3] We suggest that you write your own answers to the questions that they were asked, then turn to the bottom of page 50 to read a summary of what these religious leaders said.

   1. Does God [or your religion or spirituality] regard homosexuality as a sin?

   _____

   _____

   _____

   2. Do the Judeo-Christian Scriptures object to homosexuality?

   _____

   _____

   _____

   3. Does God [or your religion or spirituality] approve of two gay or lesbian individuals pledging love to each other in a religious ceremony and raising children born to or adopted by them?

   _____

   _____

   _____

✔ *Actively participate in your church, synagogue, mosque, or in any religious or spiritual group to which you belong.* Join the discussion. Religions are living communities that must continually debate how best to comprehend, interpret, and apply the wisdom and insights of their founders and their traditions. If you are a member, your participation is important.

What values and insights from my religious or spiritual group can help me understand and work with issues of sexual orientation?

_____

_____

_____

✔ *Take advantage of special opportunities provided by religious or spiritual affinity groups.* Many religious communities have affinity groups founded by or for their gay, lesbian, or bisexual members. These provide a special place of acceptance, spiritual nurture, and active participation in the religious community. They also help educate the larger religious community on religion and sexual orientation. Some of these groups are listed in the Resource Guide in Part 4 of this book.

Religious or spiritual resources I might want to explore:

_____

_____

_____

Opinions of Religious Leaders and Theologians

In general, the religious leaders, who came from Baptist, Episcopal, Jewish, United Methodist, Mormon, Presbyterian, Roman Catholic, United Church of Christ, and Unitarian backgrounds, were in agreement about the following:

1. God does not regard homosexuality as a sin. Individual homosexual acts, like heterosexual ones, can be loving and ethical or exploitative and selfish.

2. The Scriptures do not directly deal with what we call *homosexuality* today. They do, however, explicitly condemn institutional and individual sexual exploitation and oppression (whether heterosexual or homosexual).

3. Covenants of love and the raising of children by homosexuals as well as heterosexuals are good and sacred, provided that the partners act lovingly, unselfishly, and with respect for each other's rights and dignity.

DIVERSOPHY™

Here are a few situations drawn from *DIVERSOPHY™*, a popular training game. The questions are on this page and the answers are on page 52. If you like, you can can cut these out and use the cards as a discussion starter with friends or coworkers. More information about this game is found in the Resources section at the end of this book.

Q1.

A gay worker complains that Grace, a senior associate, has religious pictures in her office and often tells him he will burn in hell if he is not "saved." She frequently prays for him at work. As their manager, you should

A. Tell Grace that you want a religion-free workplace and to take her pictures home.

B. Transfer the gay man if possible.

C. Tell Grace that her behavior is disruptive to others and can result in disciplinary action.

Q2.

You have been working closely as a team for four months. One day, Roger tells you he overheard Mary, another team member, say, "I love you too," to an adult woman on the telephone. No one knows if Mary is a lesbian. You should

A. Do nothing. Sit on the information and tell Roger it doesn't matter.

B. "Poll" the other coworkers and get filled in on Mary.

C. Go to Mary for the truth.

Q3.

You are gay; you are offered an interior design job that is not your specialty. The project chairwoman says, "You people are so creative, and besides, we want to steal your fashion sense." You could recommend a colleague, who happens to be heterosexual. You should

A. Give her the name of your colleague. Only negative stereotypes bother you.

B. Thank her for the compliment and take the job yourself.

C. Recommend your colleague while encouraging her to drop the stereotype.

Q4.

John tells you that Rob, an openly gay co-worker, is making passes at him. John is visibly quite agitated and ready for violent behavior. As their manager, you calm John down and

A. Tell him you'll talk to Rob and discipline him if necessary.

B. Use language he'll understand: "You're too strong to worry about that little fairy."

C. Explain that he could be disciplined for hitting Rob. Promise you'll get back to him after following up on his complaint.

Here are the answers to the questions. In such human situations, there may be other, even better answers. Have you been in similar situations yourself? How well do you feel you handled them?

A2.

A. Do nothing. Sit on the information and tell Roger it doesn't matter is the best answer. Answer B. is gossiping. C. may not be welcome by Mary. She may not be ready to talk about her private life at work. Part of understanding different sexual orientations is learning that people will talk about it when they feel comfortable, and not before. Mary may even lie if she is put on the spot.

A1.

C. Tell Grace that her behavior is disruptive to others and can result in disciplinary action is the best answer. The crux of the issue is that Grace is disrupting business. Discreetly displayed personal religious items may be permissible at work. A. goes overboard and could infringe on Grace's freedom of religion. In B., the gay worker has done nothing wrong and should not be unnecessarily penalized.

A4.

C. Recommend your colleague while encouraging her to drop the stereotype is the best answer. Both A. and B. perpetuate stereotypes, even if they seem benign.

A3.

C. is best: Explain that he could be disciplined for hitting Rob. Promise you'll get back to him after following up on his complaint. The immediate danger is John's threat of violence. Do not dismiss his complaint by B., which also reinforces his homophobia, or by A., simply saying you'll handle the complaint. Many men feel threatened by homosexuals, and for some, violence is the method of handling the situation.

DIVERSE DIMENSIONS OF SEXUAL ORIENTATION

Acceptance of differences plays a great role in our ability to get along with each other and to produce results on the job. How people feel about and react to issues of sexual orientation may differ by reason of their age, ethnic background, and other cultural factors. Here are a few of these differences to be aware of when you are discussing this topic and working with people who are different from you.

Multiplicity

Remember that parts of people's identities occur simultaneously. Although we are looking at the issue of sexual orientation, this does not in any way discount the other parts of people's lives and cultures. A "typical" gay, lesbian, or bisexual person might also be black and have a physical disability. He or she may originally be from another country. Sexual orientation is just one part of the whole person. There is no single typical gay, lesbian, or bisexual person, just as there is no single model of a heterosexual.

"Gayness"

Being gay is different for every person. There is no definitive trait or expression of gayness that is the same for each person who is gay. Those variations range from differing tastes in sexual activity to types of relationships to religious beliefs to child-rearing practices, just as they do with heterosexuals.

Language, such as use of the word *queer,* may differ from generation to generation. Gays, lesbians, and bisexuals in their teens and twenties may feel more comfortable moving between sexual orientations. They might reject fixed labels. In addition, younger people may be more up-front about their identity from growing up in the gay movement of the past dozen years. However, nothing is true for everyone in any age group.

Politics

Some people think that all gay, lesbian, and bisexual people tend to be on the left of the political spectrum. However, there are several vocal and politically powerful conservative gay groups. Some gay religious groups are more traditional and strict on some matters than are mainstream religious congregations.

BISEXUALITY

Bisexuality means being attracted to people of both sexes. Although that sounds simple enough, many myths exist around the topic, as the examples below illustrate:

— Mark, paramedic: *When I came out as bisexual, my male coworkers didn't know whether they could still "bond" with me about our girlfriends.*

— Cath, illustrator: *I wonder if I say I'm in a committed relationship with someone of the opposite sex, I'll appear heterosexual.*

— Renée, medical internist: *I hate the "double closet": being rejected by both heterosexuals and gay people. Often, I don't fit in anywhere.*

— Aaron, school teacher: *I'm so tired of people telling me either "You're really straight" or "You're really gay." I'm bisexual and I always have been.*

Some Questions and Answers

❑ *Is bisexuality a phase on the way to either being gay or straight?*

For some, yes. For others, it's a permanent identity.

❑ *Do bisexuals ever settle down and marry? Are they ever completely satisfied?*

Like people of all sexual orientations, some bisexuals are in monogamous relationships. Some are married to people of the opposite sex. Some are in monogamous same-sex relationships.

❑ *Are bisexuals equally interested in both men and women?*

It differs from person to person. Some look for different things in men and women, and others say gender just isn't the determining factor in choosing a partner.

People who *call* themselves heterosexual or homosexual are often bisexual *in practice.* Many of us have been involved with people of the same sex at some time in our lives. Think now about all of the intimate experiences you have ever had. How does your experience compare to the label you currently use to describe yourself?

How You Can End Bisexual Invisibility

✓ Always include bisexuals when working on sexual orientation issues and policies.
✓ Acknowledge bisexuals' current realities and their history in the gay and lesbian movement.

TRANSGENDER ISSUES

Each of us was labeled male or female as soon as we were born. As we grew up, we were taught specific behaviors to carry out the roles of womanhood and manhood. Although many of us have felt constricted by these roles, some people feel that they were assigned the wrong role. Still others don't feel totally comfortable in either role.

Food for Thought

- ❑ When have I felt like a "real" member of my gender? What was that like?

- ❑ Have I ever felt like a member of another gender? When?

- ❑ Why do we sometimes ask, "Is that a man or a woman?" Why is it so important?

Kate Bornstein went through the expensive, lengthy, and challenging process of physically changing her body from male to female. In her book *Gender Outlaw,* she describes the requirements for what some call "sex confirmation surgery": one to two years of therapy, a lifetime of hormonal treatments, a year or two of living as another gender day and night, and then genital surgery. Although we hear about it less, about half of these operations are women becoming men.

Is This a Workplace Issue?

Yes. Because this process takes thousands of dollars, years at a time, and usually occurs in adulthood, many people who are transsexual are working people. They may change genders while on a "vacation" or during sick leave. Bornstein herself was an IBM salesperson. Often, insurance companies will pay for some or all of the treatment.

Some organizations, including a high-tech firm and a police force, have circulated a memo when an employee changed genders. This notified all staff in a clear way of what was happening, and it also let people know the employees' new names.

Who Cares Who "Pat" Is?

Society still finds it okay to laugh at people who are caught somewhere in the middle of gender roles. The *Saturday Night Live* comedy skit "It's Pat" makes fun of a person whose gender cannot be distinguished by making Pat an ugly, sniveling caricature. Creating an awareness and appreciation of transgendered people's real courage and struggles will help to lessen the bias. Seek to make the issue part of your organization's inclusion and diversity statements, policies, and training.

BECOMING ALLIES

Now that you have some new information about differing sexual orientations, the next step is to learn how to become allies for people different from yourself and to let others be allies for you.

Who is an ally?

An ally is someone who is willing to stand up and support you. Allies might have some things in common with you, but typically, they reach across difference, such as sexual orientation, to help achieve mutual goals.

What kind of person is an ally?

Allies know that their lives are richer for supporting others. They aren't threatened by people who "accuse" them of being gay or who spread rumors, because allies are secure in who they are. They know that being different is not bad, and they seek to effectively diffuse attempts to malign or slander. They are able to draw on their own experience of prejudice and unfairness to help others. They are able to see that if one group is treated unfairly, it makes it easier for another group—one they might belong to—to be mistreated. They are not allies just because it's "the right thing to do" or because they take pity on gay people. We are equal peers with those for whom we are allies, and we don't seek to "champion the cause" or outdo them in their struggle.

What do allies do?

Allies often play the valuable role of talking to people who wouldn't listen to, or even knowingly be in the company of, gay people. They get the same message of fairness out, but sometimes in words that others can better understand. Current and future heterosexual allies are already positioned in organizations where they can create change. Heterosexual allies are essential to the peaceful, productive presence of gays, lesbians, and bisexuals in the workplace.

Five Things You Can Do to Be an Effective Ally in Your Organization

1. Confront prejudiced remarks, jokes, and behaviors.

2. Encourage efforts to institute company policies that are inclusive of gay, lesbian, and bisexual concerns.

3. Treat people with whom you are allying as peers.

4. Maintain a sense of humor that degrades no one.

5. Reach out to individuals and groups to build community and coalition.

BEING ALLIES

For Heterosexuals

Being an ally is serious work. In some environments, it can mean becoming a target of physical threats and violence. Remember the legacies of courageous people who took on struggles that did not directly affect them, because to do anything less was not enough. The following list will help you to develop your skills as a heterosexual ally.[5] Reflect on these ideas and use the space below to record your thoughts either for yourself or to discuss with others.

- No matter who you are, you are the perfect person to be an ally.

- Recognize homophobia and develop creative strategies to diffuse it.

- Gays, lesbians, and bisexuals are experts on their own experiences, and you have much to learn from them. Ask, listen, and learn.

- Help where, when, and how you can.

- Be willing to take risks and make mistakes. Trust your gay, lesbian, and bisexual allies to let you.

- Learn the stories of gay, lesbian, and bisexual resistance throughout history. Help gay people to honor and celebrate the past and the present.

- Don't expect gratitude. Remember, you are an ally because you choose to be and because it is in your best interest to be. Be an ally even to those who are not willing to be yours.

- Give yourself credit for the ways in which you are able to help current and future gay, lesbian, and bisexual coworkers.

My thoughts on being or becoming an ally

_____

_____

_____

_____

_____

HAVING ALLIES

For Gay Men, Lesbians, and Bisexuals

Lesbians, gay men, and bisexuals have created one of the most diverse social and political movements in the world, spanning genders, races, nationalities, and more. But sharing perspectives with heterosexuals can be difficult for gay people because of past experiences of mistreatment. When gays, lesbians, and bisexuals have the courage to trust heterosexuals to help, however, all of our lives are that much richer and we are collectively stronger. The following items are good to keep in mind when working with heterosexual allies. Reflect on them and use the space below to record your thoughts either for yourself or to discuss with others.

- ◆ Bisexuals, lesbians, and gay men as a group, and you in particular, deserve heterosexual allies.

- ◆ Your issues are important to and affect all heterosexuals. In addition, you are the expert on your own experience.

- ◆ Heterosexuals have been hurt by homophobia themselves, and sometimes this (temporarily) prevents them from being your ally.

- ◆ Expect your heterosexual allies to be perfect allies but know they will make mistakes. Trust that they are able to deal with "difficult" issues. Tell them what you need from them.

- ◆ Gays, lesbians, and bisexuals are survivors and have a long history of resistance. Know this history and let it inspire your present challenges.

- ◆ Remember to be an ally to your allies.

My thoughts on having an ally

_____

_____

_____

_____

_____

Notes

1. Kinsey, Alfred C., Pomeroy, Wardell B., & Martin, Clyde E. (1948). *Sexual Behavior in the Human Male.* Philadelphia: W. B. Saunders.

2. *Preliminary Survey Fortune 1000 Companies on Issues of Importance to Gays, Lesbians, & Bisexuals.* (1993, October 15). (Available from the National Gay & Lesbian Task Force, Policy Institute Workplace Project, 2320 17th Street NW, Washington, DC 20009-2702; 202-332-6483)

3. Information on how to get the full results of this survey, *Is Homosexuality a Sin,* can be found in Part 4 at the end of this book.

4. DIVERSOPHY™, copyright ©1994, Multus, Inc. All rights reserved. Used by permission.

5. This list and the one under the heading *Having Allies* were developed in part by San Francisco diversity trainer Charles Seltzer.

PART 3

How Organizations Respond

Many of today's most successful organizations lead the way, not only by recognizing but by building on the potential of today's gay, lesbian, and bisexual workforce. In this section, we look at the issues such companies have faced and the steps they have taken. We will help you plan how your organization can be a more productive and friendly place not only for gays, lesbians, and bisexuals but for all of its workers by carrying out its commitment to successfully managing diversity.

IS OUR VISION BROAD ENOUGH?

It is standard practice for organizations today to articulate a vision and draft a mission statement about how they will do business or reach the goals they have set for themselves. Today's successful businesses and public agencies use such a charter to set a tone, to motivate their employees, and to tell the world their purpose and values.

On the next few pages, you will see statements from companies that have been leaders in diversity, *including the challenges raised by sexual orientation.*

Mission statements are broad and sweeping—they have to be, because diversity includes so many different kinds of people and such a wide range of issues. On the other hand, serious framers of these "organizational constitutions" insist that the inclusive words of their vision and mission be turned into policy that "puts their money where their mouth is." Later, we will discuss the many ways policy can support such a commitment. But right now, we would like you to get out a copy of your own organizational vision or mission statement and ask yourself some questions about it.

If you don't have a copy right now, use these questions to discuss your impression of the organization's values. Later, when you get a copy of your organization's mission statement, compare what you discussed with what the statement really says. If your organization has no statement, discuss your own permanent vision and mission and those of others you work with. It will help you to frame such a statement. Here is a checklist of things to ask or discuss:

If Your Organization Has a Statement	If Your Organization Does Not Have a Statement
❑ Does this statement truly include and respect all forms of diversity, including sexual orientation? How could it do this even better?	❑ What kind of wording or document would truly include and respect all forms of diversity, including sexual orientation?
❑ How well is this statement known and used in the organization?	❑ How should such a statement be created, broadcast, and used?
❑ Does it generate unanimity and excitement both about the organization's purpose and how it values its people?	❑ What kind of language must such a statement use if it is to get people's attention and commitment?
❑ What action steps have resulted from this vision?	❑ What action steps could result if such a vision and statement were in place?

Levi Strauss & Company

Mission Statement

The mission of Levi Strauss & Company is to sustain profitable and responsible commercial success by marketing jeans and selected casual apparel under the Levi's® brand.

We must balance goals of superior profitability and return on investment, leadership market positions, and superior products and service. We will conduct our business ethically and demonstrate leadership in satisfying our responsibilities to our communities and to society. Our work environment will be safe and productive and characterized by fair treatment, teamwork, open communications, personal accountability and opportunities for growth and development.

Aspiration Statement

We all want a Company that our people are proud of and committed to, where all employees have an opportunity to contribute, learn, grow and advance based on merit, not politics or background. We want our people to feel respected, treated fairly, listened to and involved. Above all, we want satisfaction from accomplishments and friendships, balanced personal and professional lives, and to have fun in our endeavors.

When we describe the kind of LS&Co. we want in the future what we are talking about is building on the foundation we have inherited: affirming the best of our Company's traditions, closing gaps that may exist between principles and practices and updating some of our values to reflect contemporary circumstances.

What Type of Leadership Is Necessary to Make Our Aspirations a Reality?

New Behaviors: Leadership that exemplifies directness, openness to influence, commitment to the success of others, willingness to acknowledge our own contributions to problems, personal accountability, teamwork and trust. Not only must we model these behaviors but we must coach others to adopt them.

Diversity: Leadership that values a diverse workforce (age, sex, ethnic group, etc.) at all levels of the organization, diversity in experience, and a diversity in perspectives. We have committed to taking full advantage of the rich backgrounds and abilities of all our people and to promote a greater diversity in positions of influence. Differing points of view will be sought; diversity will be valued and honesty rewarded, not suppressed.

Recognition: Leadership that provides greater recognition—both financial and psychic—for individuals and teams that contribute to our success. Recognition must be given to all who contribute: those who create and innovate and also those who continually support the day-to-day business requirements.

Ethical Management Practices: Leadership that epitomizes the stated standards of ethical behavior. We must provide clarity about our expectations and must enforce these standards through the corporation.

Communications: Leadership that is clear about Company, unit, and individual goals and performance. People must know what is expected of them and receive timely, honest feedback on their performance and career aspirations.

Empowerment: Leadership that increases the authority and responsibility of those closest to our products and customers. By actively pushing responsibility, trust and recognition in the organization we can harness and release the capabilities of all our people.

POLICIES AGAINST DISCRIMINATION

Mission statements are the public voice of an organization to its employees, clients, and community. Their greatest value, however, lies in the process that leads to their creation: the discussion and debate, coming to grips with the issues the mission statements represent, and forming a consensus that produces the commitment to create a new organizational culture.

An essential part of organizational policy is its stand on nondiscrimination. This is a rather simple matter on paper, but it requires a real commitment to carry it out every day. Here is an example of a simple nondiscrimination clause found in the Equal Employment Opportunity section of the policy statement of Borland International, a major developer of computer software:

> *Borland does not discriminate on the basis of race, color, religion, sex, national origin, ancestry, age, medical condition, handicap, veteran status, marital status, or sexual orientation.*

Sometimes organizations draft official stands on issues such as sexual orientation. The following is an excerpt from a larger resolution on civil rights enacted by the AFL-CIO at its 1993 convention.

Anti-Discrimination Policy of the AFL-CIO

The AFL-CIO protests any personnel actions taken against a worker solely on the basis of sexual orientation. We support enactment of legislation at all levels of government to guarantee the civil rights of all persons without regard to sexual orientation in public and private employment, housing, credit, public accommodations and public services. We also denounce harassment or violence against anyone because of his or her sexual orientation.

Affiliated unions and state and local central bodies should take an active role in opposing measures which reduce the rights of people based on their sexual orientation and should participate in appropriate coalitions in order to defeat such measures.

BROAD COMPANY SUPPORT

Many companies are undertaking a multipronged approach to supporting gay, lesbian, and bisexual issues. The following statement, named "A Commitment to Diversity," shows the different ways Coors Brewing Company in Golden, Colorado, has proudly and positively demonstrated commitment to the issue.

Coors Brewing Company

Discrimination: Coors' current Equal Employment Opportunity policy states: "It is Coors Brewing Company's policy to recruit, hire, train and promote into all job levels, employees and applicants for employment without regard to race, color, religion, sex, age, handicap, veteran status, sexual orientation or national origin."

Community Support: Coors Brewing Company and its distributors have a long history of providing support to lesbian and gay events, publications and programs. Since 1988, Coors has contributed more than $400,000 nationally to gay and lesbian organizations and activities. Also, since 1988, Coors has contributed more than $300,000 nationally to AIDS efforts.

Employee Support: As a result of the growing awareness for workplace diversity, several groups of Coors employees have formed resource councils. Among them is the Coors Lesbian and Gay Employee Resource (LAGER), a resource and advocate for lesbian and gay employees at Coors. The objectives of Coors LAGER are to:

- ♦ Be a resource to Coors on internal and external issues that affect the company and lesbian and gay employees

- ♦ Provide feedback from the company to lesbian and gay employees

- ♦ Facilitate communications between the company and the lesbian & gay community at large

- ♦ Support and empower lesbian and gay employees in their professional and personal development

- ♦ Promote a positive working environment that recognizes, rewards and values all people equally, especially in regards to hiring, company benefits and career advancement.

Contributions: Coors Brewing Company has never contributed nor plans future contributions to organizations or individuals that advocate discrimination against gays or lesbians. (The Adolph Coors Foundation is a private family foundation and is a completely separate legal entity from Coors Brewing Company.)

BIAS VERSUS POOR MANAGEMENT

Recently, a public agency called the authors' consulting company to mediate what they described as a "major diversity incident" in one of their offices. Two women had said to a gay man, "Your kind of people always thinks that way." On the surface it didn't seem to us like much more than an angry outburst and "indirect" name-calling.

When we talked to those involved, however, we found a very stressed group of workers with a demanding clientele. They had been working a daily average of four hours of unsupervised overtime for almost a month. Slurs and name-calling are always inexcusable. But stress resulting from bad management was the real culprit here, and diversity training without addressing the stress would have made the problem worse.

If your organization is full of blame for people who are different, or if name-calling is common, it is important to ask what management practices can be changed to reduce stress. Look at the quality of supervision and working conditions. How fair and reasonable are the work assignments? Does the environment add needless stress? Do people fear for their jobs?

SCAPEGOATS

Stress comes from outside the organization, too—for example, when there is a severe downturn in the economy. At such times, leaders and managers must strongly resist the general trend to find scapegoats for people's fear, disappointment, and frustration.

Jewish people, new immigrants, and, especially today, gays and lesbians have been handy targets for those who need a quick reason for why the country or the economy is "going downhill." History shows that resentful thoughts and hostile words quickly turn into real attacks on such groups. In the past twenty years, gay people have been the victims of more physical violence than any of the traditionally targeted groups in the United States.

 Historians are uncovering the story of gays and lesbians during the Nazi holocaust of the 1930s and 1940s. Forced to wear the triangle (pink for gay men, black for lesbians), they were targeted for severe abuse and eventual death in concentration camps. Today, you may see coworkers or friends wearing such triangles, which now signify gay pride and identity, honoring the suffering of the past and unifying people for a brighter future.

BLAMING THE SWUMs

Diversity management and training can also backfire when it's poorly done. For example, a program can easily increase resentment if it forcefully and falsely addresses diversity issues as if the intolerance of Straight, White, U.S.-born Men (SWUMs), or any other group, was the only cause.

Here are a few questions about scapegoating to reflect on or discuss with others:

1. What kinds of stressful situations tend to bring out resentment of others' differences for you personally? How do you handle such feelings when they arise?

2. What have been the stresses in your workplace or community when outbreaks of name-calling or even violence have occurred against gay people or other groups?

3. Do diversity efforts address everyone's prejudices and biases, or do they stack everyone else against SWUMs? Is everyone being taught how to work productively with differences, or is training focused on "fixing" one group in particular?

4. What management practices in your organization could be easily changed to reduce the amount of stress that affects people on the job?

Peer Fear

SWUMs (as well as other groups of men) also have their own work to do. For countless young men, growing up as a SWUM means learning to admire certain strong traits (usually described as "masculine" or "manly") and to fear behaviors that are classified as weak or "feminine." Peer groups enforce these values. "Peer fear" of looking "soft," coupled with misinformation about what being gay means, teaches men to avoid being seen this way at all costs. The presence of a gay man can trigger a fear in many straight men that impels them to strike out immediately in words or even actions to rid themselves of uncomfortable feelings and to be accepted by their peers.

Inadequate leaders often play on this fear. Coaches, drill sergeants, and even supervisors of all-male teams attempt to motivate men when they call them "girls," or deride the enemy or the opposing team as less than male. At work, and increasingly in schools, "sissy baiting" can be sexual harassment of the men themselves. Truly strong men, straight or gay, are comfortable with all kinds of people, as are strong women. As one man put it, "Working with gay men on a day-to-day basis made me see how important it was to manage my own fears. I'm a lot stronger now because I know and accept myself better. I accept others better, too."

Good managers make it hard for peer fear to set in. They help workers to see their own limitations. Such managers, simply by being good role models, do a lot to make diversity programs successful.

"OUT" IN CORPORATE AMERICA

What happens to an organization if it publicly comes out in support of its gay, lesbian, and bisexual employees? What should it watch out for? Here are some questions commonly asked by boards of directors, chief executives, and senior managers along with some suggested ways to respond to them:

Q. *Won't paying public attention to these issues cause confusion and division?*

A. Probably no more than any other organizational change. If you are publicly announcing your commitment to this new level of equity and productivity, you must have thought it through and be ready to implement it throughout the organization. People inside and outside the organization must know what the company is doing and why it is doing it.

Q. *Isn't this inviting trouble from people who hate gays?*

A. Chances are that you will get some negative reaction. It is usually motivated by fear. Respond wherever possible by accepting people's fears and being confident that you can work them out. Resistance normally lasts only a short time. It disappears when it becomes clear that you mean business and are not about to back off from your commitment. If you encounter a stronger reaction that becomes a threat to your business, such as a boycott or property damage, reaffirm your commitment to your goals and take whatever legal measures are within your rights.

Q. *What will our customers think? Won't we lose some contracts?*

A. Your customers are primarily concerned about the quality and reliability of your products and services. They want solid working relationships and good customer service from your representatives. Creating support for all of your workers will increase their ability to serve your customers better. You should eventually gain contracts, not lose them.

Q. *Couldn't one of our high-level people be blackmailed or blacklisted from sources of crucial information in the field if she or he "came out"?*

A. Historically, the risk of blackmail seems to be higher when high-ranking gays, lesbians, and bisexuals are closeted. Prejudice and bias do exist, and blacklisting or social rejection are possible on occasions, but this is getting harder to do, especially if such practices are revealed or made public. The North American sense of fair play is an important counterweight to our biases. If the organization and its leaders are united in their decisions and show up as allies when one of their number is attacked, little damage, if any, is likely to occur.

Q. *Should I appoint a gay person to represent our company at important meetings and events?*

A. Only if he or she is the best person for the job.

POLICIES AND POLITICS—
What Do We Need to Know?

No company wants to be caught in the uncomfortable bind of a court case like that portrayed in the movie *Philadelphia,* in which a gay lawyer with AIDS sued his firm—and won—after being unjustly fired. Ironically, the people that Tom Hanks's character faced in court were a group of senior lawyers who should have been aware of federal, state, and city policies on sexual orientation and HIV infection and AIDS.

As any human resource manager knows, organizations must abide by federal, state, and municipality labor codes, laws, and ordinances as well as by company policy. Eight states have civil rights laws protecting gays and lesbians that have been passed by their legislatures and signed by the governors:

California (1992)	Minnesota (1993)
Connecticut (1991)	New Jersey (1992)
Hawaii (1991)	Vermont (1992)
Massachusetts (1989)	Wisconsin (1982)

In addition to the above list, at the time of this publication, at least eighteen states have executive orders from their governors, at least eighty-seven cities or counties in the United States have civil rights ordinances, and at least thirty-nine cities or counties in the United States have council or mayoral proclamations banning discrimination in public employment.

This sample comes from a Washington, D.C., local ordinance:

"It shall be an unlawful discriminatory practice to do any of the following acts, wholly or partially for a discriminatory reason based upon race, color, religion, national origin, sex, age, marital status, personal appearance, sexual orientation, family responsibilities, physical handicap, matriculation, or political affiliation, of any individual; . . . to refuse to hire, or to discharge . . . [to] fail to initiate or conduct any transaction in real property . . . to deny, directly or indirectly, any person the full and equal enjoyment of the goods, services, facilities, privileges, advantages, and accommodations of any place or public accommodation; . . . to deny . . . access to, any of [an educational institution's] facilities and services . . ."

According to Oakland, California, employment lawyer Patti Roberts, cases are coming through the courts now that are setting precedents for employment law and sexual orientation.

How can an organization stay on top of the legal changes? Roberts says that companies with explicit regulations have fewer conflicts related to sexual orientation, HIV infection, and AIDS. Below are some important legal facts with which all organizations should be familiar, along with some recommendations on how to best deal with them:

> **Fact:** You are required to know and observe the antidiscrimination ordinances and laws in your city, county, state, and at the federal level. These are too numerous and varied to even summarize here.

> **Fact:** According to these laws, you and your organization may be liable for the inappropriate behavior of your employees, contract personnel, vendors, and customers.

We recommend the following:

✓ *Have a clearly written company policy* on sexual orientation discrimination either as a separate item or as a part of a larger nondiscrimination policy. Do this with both legal counsel and in consultation with any gay, lesbian, or bisexual employee groups that exist.

✓ *Distribute the policy* in such a way that all managers and employees are aware of its existence and intent.

✓ *Train managers and supervisors.* Each should not only know the law but be instructed and trained in how to apply it—for example, how to handle conflicts and complaints that may occur. This book can be the basis of such a program.

✓ *Train employees.* Training should help employees deal with homophobia and behaviors that result from bias. Track whether employees have been through this training to ensure that each individual in the company has received the message.

✓ *Encourage the creation of gay, lesbian, or bisexual affinity groups* if they do not exist, just as you would encourage other groups whose situation or special concerns affect the quality of workers' lives. These groups can advise you on their situation in the workplace and needs that arise.

HIV, AIDS, AND THE WORKPLACE

This is a book about sexual orientation. But because HIV infection and AIDS have had a profound effect on gays, lesbians, and bisexuals, and because so many stereotypes still exist about the disease and are played out in the workplace, we need to give the topic special attention here.

Many people have deep fears about this terrifying health crisis, now in its second decade. Ideally, people should come together and confront their fears with solid information. Unfortunately, what is happening now in many places fosters fear, hatred, and separation, which can lead to scapegoating. With positive, compassionate steps designed for everyone, organizations can set standards of equity and lead the way in establishing tolerance and understanding.

We recommend that businesses create policies on HIV and AIDS. At least a third of U.S. businesses have such policies, such as Wells Fargo Bank, the AFL-CIO, and Syntex, Inc. Many helpful AIDS organizations are listed in the Resource section.

What Is HIV and AIDS?

AIDS means *acquired immunodeficiency syndrome*. It is caused by the human immunodeficiency virus, or HIV. There is no cure and no vaccination. HIV weakens the body's natural ability to fight diseases. As the immune system fails, a person may develop life-threatening illnesses, called "opportunistic infections," such as pneumonia and cancer. The presence of HIV and one of these opportunistic infections is necessary for a person to be officially diagnosed with AIDS.

HIV-infected people, however, may not show signs of illness for many years and will continue to be productive members of the workforce. They have the same rights and opportunities as people with other serious or life-threatening illnesses.

One of Every 150

The Center for Disease Control reports that 2 million people in the United States are infected with HIV, or one out of every 150 people. The majority of those people are between the ages of 25 and 44, the nation's present and future workforce. Worldwide, more than 3 million people have died from AIDS, and over 13 million people are infected with HIV right now.

The increasing numbers of people with HIV, and now their longer life expectancy, will result in more people on the job with HIV. This means that the spread of HIV and AIDS will affect you, whether you are a business owner, manager, or employee.

WRITE A WORKPLACE HIV POLICY

Your workplace policy should at least address the following:

❑ Compliance with federal, state, and local antidiscrimination laws, the Americans with Disabilities Act of 1990, the Federal Rehabilitation Act of 1973, and the Occupational Safety and Health Administration (OSHA) guidelines about infection control procedures and establishing written exposure control plans to protect workers

❑ Hiring, promotion, transfer, and dismissal policies with regard to employees and potential employees with HIV and AIDS

❑ Maintaining confidentiality of employee medical records and information

❑ Defining ways that management will address workplace discrimination

❑ Promoting prevention and understanding through employee education

❑ Deciding who will be trained on this information and how

❑ Designing an employee support group for people with HIV and AIDS and their supporters at work

Educate Employees

Education is the best way to stop the spread of HIV and AIDS. By replacing myths with facts, fears of coworkers and customers will lessen. You can do the following:

♦ Offer seminars, with basic facts about HIV infection and AIDS, with people from outside your organization to address employees' questions and fears.

♦ Distribute payroll inserts and brochures on HIV prevention for your employees and their families.

♦ Display informational posters in the workplace about HIV and AIDS.

♦ Show prevention videos at company meetings and training programs.

Volunteer to Help

1. Have a representative serve as liaison to community councils and groups concerned with the issue.

2. Donate your firm's services or materials to local HIV and AIDS organizations.

3. Have volunteers from your organization directly help people with HIV and AIDS.

4. Participate in and support school education programs.

5. Collect material donations, raise money, or participate in local AIDS organizations' events.

A Nondiscrimination Checklist

Are you able to say "yes" to each of the following questions? If not, you still have some work to do to meet the minimum standards for an effective nondiscrimination policy.

❑ Yes, we have a policy to provide a working environment that is not only free of sexual harassment for employees regardless of their sexual orientation but that also forbids harassment of people specifically because of their sexual orientation.

❑ Yes, rumors and complaints of harassment of gay people are promptly and thoroughly looked into by the responsible level of authority.

❑ Yes, we take prompt and effective disciplinary action when it is called for.

❑ Yes, our employees feel free to report incidents and concerns without fear of retaliation.

AIDS AND THE LAW

As we have stressed elsewhere, AIDS is not specifically a disease of gay men. It has, however, strongly attacked that population in the United States, and many people still tend to identify it as a "gay disease." Therefore we give it special attention here.

> **Fact:** People with HIV infection and AIDS are protected by the Americans with Disabilities Act of 1990. This means that the employment rights of people who suffer from permanent impairment of a major life function, as well as their caregivers, are protected in all organizations of fifteen or more employees. Local laws may be even more stringent. You cannot fire without good cause someone infected with HIV or, for example, refuse to hire the spouse, relative, or friend of a person with AIDS because you believe that the caregiver won't be able to bear the workload.

> **Fact:** People who are perceived to have HIV or AIDS, even mistakenly, are also protected. For example, if you assume that a frail-looking individual has AIDS, that person is automatically covered by the law whether or not she or he actually has the virus.

SEXUAL HARASSMENT CONCERNS

Does the coexistence of people with various sexual orientations in the workplace raise a special concern about sexual harassment? The answer, technically and legally, is a clear "No." In the minds and feelings of many people, however, there is confusion about sexual harassment and sexual orientation. Some people assume that the presence of bisexuals, lesbians, and gay men on the job will cause special problems.

These facts should be clearly understood by all. Check any of those that you feel need to be better known or understood in your organization:

❑ *Sexual harassment legislation and policy are the same for all, whatever their sexual orientation.* This means that anyone who harasses another, whether the victim is of the other sex or of the same sex, is out of line, and appropriate remedies must be taken.

❑ *There is no evidence that gay people are more inclined to abuse* power over others, more likely to be involved in workplace romance, use sexual talk more frequently, and so on than individuals of any other group. In some cases, a lesbian or gay person who is "out of the closet" has a higher profile and may be more noticed if she or he engages in truly inappropriate behavior.

❑ Sometimes friendliness and casual conversational touching, *when done by known gay people, are given a different interpretation* than if they were done by straight individuals. Everyday gestures can be invested with more meaning than they really have. In a multicultural workplace, there are many challenges of this kind to sort out. People from some backgrounds will give signals that seem overly intimate to people from other cultural groups. Our discomforts with each other need to be surfaced and talked out before they are blown out of proportion.

❑ *Sexual harassment issues may themselves be out of hand.* In an organization where lawsuits and complaints are common, where relations between the sexes are strained and highly politicized, where allegations of sexual harassment and fears of such allegations are increasing, anything having to do with gender or sexual orientation calls attention to itself. This makes gay people, in particular, vulnerable, and they can become pawns in the political struggles of others.

DOMESTIC PARTNER BENEFITS

Many organizations are now expanding the benefits they offer to married heterosexuals and their families to include partners of gays and lesbians. In some cases, unmarried partners of heterosexual employees can participate in these plans, which typically include medical and health insurance, bereavement leave, family leave, and more.

Requirements to be classified as a domestic partner vary slightly from organization to organization. In general, the required items include a statement or affidavit by two adults affirming that they are in a committed partnership, are each other's sole domestic partners, share the common necessities of life, and are responsible for each other's welfare.

If you are considering bringing domestic partner benefits to your organization, we recommend that you contact the list of Domestic Partnership Resources in Part 4. The National Gay & Lesbian Task Force, a Washington, D.C., lobbying and information organization, offers a *Domestic Partners Organizing Manual.* Another resource is the *Stanford Report on Domestic Partner Benefits,* which provides a cost analysis that is useful for both employees and management.

On the next few pages, we have listed organizations and municipalities that offer domestic partner benefits as part of their employee benefits package. This information was supplied by the National Gay & Lesbian Task Force and other sources. More and more organizations in different fields and across the country are choosing to offer these benefits to employees.

By offering domestic partner benefits, these organizations let gay, lesbian, bisexual, and heterosexual employees know that all employees' home lives and work lives are important and worth supporting. These benefits go far in attracting and retaining the best workers, regardless of sexual orientation.

Does your firm offer domestic partner benefits to gays and lesbians? _____

Does it offer these benefits to unmarried heterosexual couples? _____

If your organization does not offer these benefits, what needs to happen so that it does? What information do you need? Who needs to be vocal? Who needs to be listened to?

_____

_____

More than sixty **companies and public agencies** now offer domestic partner benefits to gay and lesbian employees, including the following:

Adobe Systems, Sunnyvale, CA

AT&T, New York, NY

Ask/Ingres, San Mateo, CA

Apple Computer, Cupertino, CA

Autodesk, Inc., Sausalito, CA

Bank of America, San Francisco, CA

Banyan Systems, Westboro, MA

Bay Area Rapid Transit, San Francisco, CA

Bell-Northern Research, Canada

Ben & Jerry's Homemade, Inc., Waterbury, VT

Berkeley Unified School District, Berkeley, CA

Beth Israel Medical Center, New York, NY

Borland International, Scotts Valley, CA

Boston Children's Hospital, Boston, MA

The Boston Globe, Boston, MA

Blue Cross and Blue Shield of Massachusetts, Boston, MA

Cadence, San Jose, CA

California Pacific Medical Center, San Francisco, CA

Chiron Corporation, Emeryville, CA

Consumer United Insurance Company, Washington, DC

Dane Regional Planning Commission, Dane County, WI

DEC-Belgium, Boston, MA

Fannie Mae, Washington, DC

Fred Hutchinson Cancer Research Center, Seattle, WA

Frame Technology, Boston, MA

Gardner's Supply Company, Burlington, VT

Genentech, Inc., South San Francisco, CA

Golston & Storrs, Attorneys at Law, Boston, MA

Group Health Cooperative, Seattle, WA

Home Box Office, New York, NY

Interleaf, Boston, MA

International Data Group, Framingham, MA

Kaiser Permanente, Oakland, CA

Levi Strauss Corporation, San Francisco, CA

Lotus Development Corporation, Cambridge, MA

MCA/Universal, Hollywood, CA

Microsoft, Inc., Seattle, WA

Milbank, Tweed, Hadley & McCloy, New York, NY

Mintz, Levin & Ferris, Boston, MA

Montefiore Medical Center, New York, NY

NeXT Computer, Redwood City, CA

Oracle Corporation, Redwood City, CA

Orrick, Herrington & Sutcliffe, San Francisco, CA

Pacific Gas & Electric Company, San Francisco, CA

Quark, Inc., Boulder, CO

Para Transit, Inc., Sacramento, CA

Sage Publications, Inc., Thousand Oaks, CA

Santa Cruz Transit District, Santa Cruz, CA

Seattle Mental Health Institute, Seattle, WA

Seattle Times, Seattle, WA

The Segal Company, Boston, MA

Shiff, Harden & Waite, Chicago, IL

Silicon Graphics, Inc., Mountain View, CA

Sprint, Westwood, KN

Sun Microsystems, Milpitas, CA

SuperMac Technologies, Sunnyvale, CA

Starbucks Coffee, Seattle, WA

Sybase, Inc., Berkeley, CA

Thinking Machines Company, Cambridge, MA

Time, Inc., New York, NY

Village Voice, New York, NY

Warner Brothers Pictures, Hollywood, CA

Woodward & Lothrop, Inc., Washington, DC

Xerox Corporation, Stamford, CT

Ziff Davis Publishing, New York, NY

Domestic partner benefits are offered at about thirty **colleges, universities, and professional schools**, including the following:

Albert Einstein College of Medicine, New York, NY	Simmons College, Boston, MA
American University, Washington, DC	Smith College, Northampton, MA
Clark University, Worcester, MA	Stanford University, Palo Alto, CA
Colby College, Waterville, ME	Swarthmore College, Swarthmore, PA
Columbia University, New York, NY	University of Chicago, Chicago, IL
Cornell University, Ithaca, NY	University of Colorado, Boulder, CO
Harvard University, Cambridge, MA	University of Iowa, Iowa City, IA
Massachusetts Institute of Technology, Cambridge, MA	University of Minnesota, Minneapolis, MN
Middlebury College, Middlebury, VT	University of Pennsylvania, Philadelphia, PA
Mount Holyoke College, South Hadley, MA	University of Vermont, Burlington, VT
Pitzer College, Claremont, CA	University of Wisconsin, Madison, WI
Pomona College, Pomona, CA	Wellesley College, Wellesley, MA
Princeton University, Princeton, NJ	Wesleyan University, Middletown, CT
	Williams College, Williamstown, MA
	Yale University, New Haven, CT

Nearly twenty **not-for-profit organizations** offer domestic partner benefits:

American Civil Liberties Union, San Francisco, CA	Los Angeles Philharmonic, Los Angeles, CA
American Friends Service Committee, Philadelphia, PA	Minnesota Communications Group/Minnesota Public Radio, St. Paul, MN
American Psychological Association, Washington, DC	Museum of Modern Art, New York, NY
Consumer's Union, San Francisco, CA	National Center for Lesbian Rights, San Francisco, CA
Episcopal Church of Newark, Newark, NJ	National Gay & Lesbian Task Force, Washington, DC
Greenpeace International, Washington, DC	National Organization for Women, Washington, DC
Human Rights Campaign Fund, Washington, DC	National Public Radio, Washington, DC
KQED Radio, San Francisco, CA	Planned Parenthood Association, New York, NY
Lambda Legal Defense & Education Fund, New York, NY	Union of American Hebrew Congregations, Washington, DC

Nearly forty **municipalities, the State of Vermont,** and **the State of Massachusetts** offer domestic partner benefits to their employees:

Alameda County, CA	Multnomah County, OR
Ann Arbor, MI	New Orleans, LA
Baltimore, MD	New York, NY
Berkeley, CA	Oak Park, IL
Boston, MA	Oakland, CA
Brookline, MA	Rochester, NY
Burlington, VT	Sacramento, CA
Cambridge, MA	Santa Cruz, CA
Chicago, IL	Santa Cruz County, CA
Dane County, WI	San Francisco, CA
East Lansing, MI	San Matteo County, CA
Hartford, CT	Seattle, WA
Hennepin County, MN	Shorewood Hills Village, WI
Ithaca, NY	State of Vermont
King County, WA	Takoma Park, MD
Laguna Beach, CA	Travis County, TX
Los Angeles, CA	Washington, DC
Madison, WI	West Hollywood, CA
Marin County, CA	West Palm Beach, FL
Minneapolis, MN	

BEST PRACTICES

On the next several pages, you will find a list of "best practices"—actions that various organizations have found successful in working with sexual orientation issues. They are arranged so that you can work with them and discuss them with others. You can use the box on the left to check the items that you think would be possible or desirable in your organization. Then, use the space on the right to note such things as the first steps you might want to take, who you might want to talk to about this, or expected obstacles.

A. What Employers and Management Do

Best Practices	Notes
❑ Have the CEO and heads of the organization say that they expect 100% from their employees and therefore employees can expect 100% support from them.	
❑ Have senior management meet with all affinity groups.	
❑ Have Human Resources include information about the gay, lesbian, and bisexual group in the employee orientation packet.	
❑ Add sexual orientation to the company's nondiscrimination clause.	
❑ Alter language in all company announcements and statements so that gay men, lesbians, and bisexuals, along with their partners and families, are included.	
❑ Establish a benefits package for employees' domestic partners.	
❑ Be present at gay, lesbian, and bisexual community events, especially business networking opportunities. Raise money for AIDS-related causes.	
❑ Endorse diversity training for all employees on bias and sexual orientation. Shape the training into a brainstorming session on marketing, outreach, and business opportunities.	

B. What Gay, Lesbian, and Bisexual Employee Groups Do

Best Practices	Notes
❑ Use the experiences of gay groups at other firms. Don't reinvent the wheel.	
❑ Send multiple messages to different levels of the organization.	
❑ Be a group any way you can. Go inside and outside the firm, on-site and off-site.	
❑ Invite the entire company to your functions.	
❑ Get an inexpensive 800 number for communicating across the corporation.	
❑ Keep your mailing list private. Mark everything "personal and confidential."	
❑ Create a nonthreatening allies workshop for SWUMs and other heterosexuals.	
❑ Get approval for a gay, lesbian, and bisexual group T-shirt with the company logo.	
❑ Support other affinity groups' issues, and they will support you.	
❑ Support the work management does to support you. Supply them with information they need to enact domestic partners' benefits and other measures.	
❑ Bring your issues to your union. Have it take on your struggles.	
❑ Participate in gay community celebrations as representatives of your firm.	

C. What Individual Employees Do

Best Practices	Notes
❑ Don't let your fear get in the way of what you believe. Rely on allies to help.	
❑ Ask for commitment and concrete "next steps" from management and other group members.	
❑ Let people be effective where they can.	
❑ Find safe, useful means of communication between yourself and others, such as confidential and electronic mail.	

D. Our/My Best Practices

Lists of best practices, such as we've noted here, come from looking at and writing down what people do that is effective. Even if your organization has not consciously begun to deal with sexual orientation issues, there are probably groups and individuals who have had some success in doing so because of the way they think, behave, and handle situations. Perhaps there are some things that you personally have done that have worked well. Use the space at the right to create a list of these. Ask others to brainstorm a list of the best practices they see or personally use. Share and compare lists.

1. _____

_____

_____

_____

2. _____

_____

_____

_____

3. _____

_____

_____

_____

4. _____

_____

_____

_____

A $500 BILLION MARKET

There's a marketing secret worth $500 billion: the gay, lesbian, and bisexual market. Although many of the estimated 5 to 20 million people who fit that category aren't out of the closet, all of them purchase goods and services in this country and have a combined income of approximately $500 billion each year.

Research reported by Marlene Rossman, author of *Multicultural Marketing,* shows that gay men have an average annual income of $52,000, and lesbians have an average of $43,000. One reason is that these groups tend to be "DINKS," households with dual incomes and no kids, although the gay family configuration is changing. With more than 40% of this population earning more than $60,000, these individuals, on average, have large disposable incomes. Although some research disputes these findings, the number of gay consumers is undeniably huge.

What does your organization do or produce that could be marketed specifically to gay men, lesbians, and bisexuals? Have any steps been taken in this direction?

_____

_____

_____

_____

_____

_____

Successful Advertisers

Firms such as The Gap, Phillip Morris, Absolut Vodka, Time Warner, Calvin Klein, and American Express have taken advantage of this market through advertising in gay and lesbian publications such as *Out, Deneuve,* and *The Advocate.* Such gay-targeted ads are not necessarily a political statement, they're simply good business: *The Advocate* reaches 68,000 people. Also, gay, lesbian, and bisexual customers tend to be loyal to companies and brand names. Remember that gay people get hit at least twice by advertising messages: once through the mainstream and a second time through the gay media.

This is a win-win situation for both advertisers and the gay, lesbian, and bisexual market because gays feel acknowledged, respected, and supported when a major firm values their buying power. They want to see positive images of themselves in mainstream advertisements for Fortune 500 companies' products or notice a major company's ad in a gay, lesbian, or bisexual publication.

How to Enter This Market

How can your organization tap into this advertisers' pot of gold? Along with Marlene Rossman, we suggest these steps:

♦ Advertise in gay and lesbian media.

♦ Sponsor, support, and contribute to gay community events, including AIDS-related causes, and gay, lesbian, and bisexual employee business networking events.

♦ Encourage your gay, lesbian, and bisexual employees' group to give your company free advertising at Gay Pride marches by carrying a banner with your logo.

Another good advertisement, of course, is to be known as a company that treats employees of all sexual orientations decently and fairly. Word will travel fast in gay, lesbian, and bisexual communities and among their allies, and it will not soon be forgotten.

Think about how your company or agency serves the gay, lesbian, and bisexual population. How can it reach out more directly and more profitably? What kind of marketing or outreach to the gay, lesbian, and bisexual community could you undertake? What might your organization do next?

_____

_____

_____

_____

The questions on page 89 ask how your organization can realize the potential that the gay, lesbian, and bisexual community represents. You may want to organize a sales and marketing meeting among your staff to specifically address this issue. Or you could explore organizational opportunities in the last segment of an awareness training on sexual orientation.

As a training exercise, break into small groups and examine the different development, marketing, and outreach possibilities this issue presents to your company or agency. The results of this collective brainstorming session can be tremendous.

PART 4

The Gay, Lesbian, and Bisexual Resource Directory

Here are some useful sources of information on the topic of sexual orientation for you as an individual and as a member of an organization. There are thousands of helpful groups and warehouses of information on this subject, far too many to list here. We also encourage you to call on your local resources whenever possible. We hope you use this directory to continue the work you have begun in these pages.

BOOKS AND ARTICLES

Adam, Barry D. (1987). *The Rise of a Gay and Lesbian Movement.* Boston: Twayne.

Baker, D. B., Strub, Sean O'Brien, & Henning, Bill, in association with the National Gay & Lesbian Task Force. (1995). *Cracking the Corporate Closet: The 200 Best (and Worst) Companies to Work for, Buy From, and Invest In.* New York: Harper Business.

Be Yourself: Questions & Answers for Gay, Lesbian, and Bisexual Youth. (Booklet available from P-FLAG, 1-800-4-FAMILY)

Beck, E. T. (Ed.). (1982). *Nice Jewish Girls: A Lesbian Anthology.* Trumensburg, NY: Crossing Press.

Bell, Alan P., Weinberg, Martin S., & Hammersmith, Sue Kiefer. (1981). *Sexual Preference: Its Development in Men and Women.* Bloomington: Indiana University Press.

Berubé, Alan. (1994). *Coming Out Under Fire: The History of Gay Men and Women in World War II.* New York: New American Library.

Berzon, Betty. (1988). *Permanent Partners: Building Gay and Lesbian Relationships That Last.* New York: E. P. Dutton.

Blumenfeld, Warren J., & Raymond, Dave. (1988). *Looking at Gay and Lesbian Life.* Boston: Beacon.

Bornstein, Kate. (1995). *Gender Outlaw.* New York: Vintage.

Boswell, John. (1980). *Christianity, Social Tolerance and Homosexuality.* Chicago: University of Chicago Press.

Brenner, Claudia. (1995). *Eight Bullets: One Woman's Story of Surviving Anti-Gay Violence.* Ithaca, NY: Firebrand.

Cowan, Thomas. (1992). *Gay Men and Women Who Enriched the World.* Boston: Alyson.

Curb, R., & Manahan, N. (1985). *Lesbian Nuns: Breaking Silence.* New York: Warner.

Deevey, Sharon. (1993). Lesbian Self-Disclosure: Strategies for Success. *Journal of Psychosocial Nursing, 16*(5), 35-39.

D'Emilio, John. (1983). *Sexual Politics, Sexual Communities: The Making of a Homosexual Minority in the United States, 1940-1970.* Chicago: University of Chicago Press.

Frank, Miriam, & Holcomb, Desma. (1990). *Pride at Work: Organizing for Lesbian and Gay Rights in Unions.* New York: Lesbian and Gay Labor Network.

Garwood, Anne, & Melnick, Ben. (1995). *What Everyone Can Do to Fight AIDS.* San Francisco, CA: Jossey-Bass.

Geller, Thomas (Ed.). (1990). *Bisexuality: A Reader and Source Book.* Ojai, CA: Times Change Press.

Grahn, Judy. (1984). *Another Mother Tongue.* Boston: Beacon.

Hall, M. (1986). The Lesbian Corporate Experience. *Journal of Homosexuality, 12*(3/4), 59-75.

Herek, Gregory M. (1986). The Social Psychology of Homophobia: Toward a Practical Theory. *New York University Review of Law & Social Change, 14(4), 923-934.*

Human Rights Foundation. (1984). *Demystifying Homosexuality: A Teaching Guide About Lesbians and Gay Men.* New York: Irvington.

Is Homosexuality a Sin? (Booklet available from P-FLAG, 1-800-4-FAMILY)

Kaahumanu, Lani, & Hutchins, Lorraine (Eds.). (1990). *Bi Any Other Name: Bisexual People Speak Out.* Boston: Alyson.

Katz, Jonathan. (1976). *Gay American History.* New York: Avon.

Kepner, Jim. (1983). *Becoming a People: A Four Thousand Year Gay and Lesbian Chronology.* West Hollywood, CA: National Gay Archives.

Kinsey, Alfred C., Pomeroy, Wardell B., & Martin, Clyde E. (1948). *Sexual Behavior in the Human Male.* Philadelphia: W. B. Saunders.

Kinsey, Alfred C., Pomeroy, Wardell B., Martin, Clyde E., & Gebhard, Paul H. (1953). *Sexual Behavior in the Human Female.* Philadelphia: W. B. Saunders.

Kronenberger, George K. (1991, June). Out of the Closet. *Personnel Journal,* pp. 40-44.

Leinen, Stephen. (1993). *Gay Cops.* New Brunswick, NJ: Rutgers University Press.

Less Equal Than Others: A Survey of Lesbians and Gay Men at Work. (Survey conducted in England, available from Stonewall, 2 Greycoat Place, London, SW1P 1SB, UK)

Levine, M. P., & Leonard, R. (1984). Discrimination Against Lesbians in the Work Force. *Signs, 9*(4), 700-710.

Liebowitch, Jacques. (1985). *A Strange Virus of Unknown Origin.* New York: Ballantine.

Marmor, Judd. (1980). *Homosexual Behavior—A Modern Reappraisal.* New York: Basic Books.

Martin, A. D. (1982). Learning to Hide: The Socialization of the Gay Adolescent. In S. C. Feinstein, J. G. Looney, A. Schwartzburg, & A. Sorsky (Eds.), *Adolescent Psychiatry: Developmental and Clinical Studies* (Vol. 10, pp. 52-65). Chicago: University of Chicago Press.

Masters, William, & Johnson, Virginia. (1979). *Homosexuality in Perspective.* Boston: Little, Brown.

Mckinley, Catherine E., & DeLaney, L. Joyce. (1995). *Afrekete.* New York: Anchor.

McNaught, Brian. (1993). *Gay Issues in the Workplace.* New York: St. Martin's.

Media Guide to the Lesbian and Gay Community. (1990). Gay and Lesbian Alliance Against Defamation (GLAAD). (150 West 26th Street, Suite 503, New York, NY 10001).

Miller, Neil. (1995). *Gay and Lesbian History From 1869 to the Present.* New York: Vintage.

Moulding, Karen. (Ed.). (1995). *Sexual Orientation and the Law* (7th ed., National Lawyers Guild Lesbian, Gay, Bisexual Rights Committee.) New York: Clark, Boardman, Callaghan. (1-800-221-9428)

Newman, Leslea. (1995). *A Loving Testimony: Remembering Loved Ones Lost to AIDS.* Watsonville, CA: Crossing Press.

Phariss, Tracy. (1994). *A Bibliography: Gay and Lesbian Issues in Education.* (Available from the Teachers' Group of Colorado, P.O. Box 280346, Lakewood, CO 80228-0346)

Plant, Richard. (1986). *Pink Triangle.* New York: Henry Holt.

Powers, Bob, & Ellis, Alan. (1993). *America's Guide to Gay, Lesbian and Bisexual Workplace Issues.* San Francisco: Bob Powers Publications.

Resolution passed in 1973 by the American Psychiatric Association Board of Trustees. National Gay & Lesbian Task Force: Gay Civil Rights Support Statements and Resolutions Packet. (1-202-332-6483)

Rutledge, Leigh W. (1987). *The Gay Book of Lists.* Boston: Alyson.

Schmitz, T. J. (1988). Career Counseling Implications With the Gay and Lesbian Population. *Journal of Employment Counseling, 25*(2), 51-56.

Schneider, B. E. (1987). Coming Out at Work: Bridging the Private/Public Gap. *Work & Occupations, 13*(4), 463-487.

Sexual Orientation: An Issue of Workforce Diversity (Ad hoc report, U.S. Department of Agriculture Forest Service). (1992). (Available from USDA-Forest Service, Pacific Southwest Region, Office of Civil Rights, 630 Sansome Street, San Francisco, CA 94111)

Shilts, Randy. (1977). *The Mayor of Castro Street.* New York: St. Martin's.

Shilts, Randy. (1982). *And the Band Played On.* New York: St. Martin's.

Shilts, Randy. (1994). *Conduct Unbecoming: Gays & Lesbians in the U.S. Military.* New York: Fawcett Columbine.

Signorile, Michaelangelo. (1995). *Outing Yourself: How to Come Out to Your Family, Your Friends, and Your Coworkers.* New York: Random House.

Stewart, Thomas A. (1991, December 16). Gay in Corporate America. *Fortune,* pp. 42-56.

Thompson, Mark. (Ed.). (1994). *Long Road to Freedom: The Advocate History of the Gay and Lesbian Movement.* New York: St. Martin's.

Wallace, Amy, Wallace, Irving, & Wallechinsky, David. (1977). Sixty-Seven Renowned Homosexuals and Bisexuals. *The People's Almanac Presents the Book of Lists.* New York: William Morrow.

Woods, James. (1993). *The Corporate Closet.* New York: Free Press.

FILMS AND VIDEOS (Listed by Distributor)

Cambridge Documentary Films, P.O. Box 385, Cambridge, MA 02139, 617-354-3677.

♦ *Pink Triangles.* Documentary exploring prejudice against lesbians and gay men through personal interviews.

Cinema Guild, 1697 Broadway, Suite 506, New York, NY 10019-5904, 212-246-5522.

♦ *Before Stonewall: The Making of a Gay and Lesbian Community.* Emmy Award-winning documentary on the history of gays and lesbians in the United States.

Equity Institute, 6400 Hollis Street, Suite 15, Emeryville, CA 94608, 510-658-4577.

♦ *Sticks, Stones and Stereotypes.* (1988). Video focusing on verbal harassment and homophobia and the relation of homophobia to other bigotries. Accompanied by a Spanish and English curriculum guide of the same name.

Excellence in Training, 11358 Aurora Avenue, Des Moines, IA 50322, 800-747-6569.

♦ *Gay Issues in the Workplace.* Brian McNaught discusses pros and cons of "coming out," the benefits of an employee support group, and the effects of gay-friendly company policies.

♦ *Homophobia in the Workplace.* Brian McNaught defines homophobia and how it undermines morale and productivity. He illuminates obstacles that gays and lesbians face at work.

Parents and Friends of Lesbians and Gays, P.O. Box 18901, Denver, CO 80218, 303-333-0286.

♦ *An Unexpected Journey.* A series of narratives and interviews shows what it is like to be gay or lesbian and to be the parent of a gay or lesbian person.

Telling Pictures Distribution, 2300 Market Street, #121, San Francisco, CA 94114, 415-864-6714.

♦ *The Times of Harvey Milk.* Academy Award-winning documentary about the life and death of openly gay San Francisco City Supervisor Harvey Milk.

TRB Productions, P.O. Box 2362, Boston, MA 02107, 617-236-7800.

♦ *On Being Gay.* Author and lecturer Brian McNaught speaks about the fallacies, facts, and feelings of being gay in a straight world. Eighty-minute presentation for viewing in forty-minute segments.

Woman Vision Productions, 3145 Geary Boulevard, Box 421, San Francisco, CA 94118, 415-346-2336.

♦ *Straight From the Heart.* Parents' struggles with homophobia after learning that their child is lesbian or gay, and their journey to a new understanding.

♦ *Out for a Change: Homophobia in Women's Sports.* Video exposes devastating emotional effect of homophobia on all women athletes. Includes interviews with college student athletes, coaches, National Collegiate Athletic Association (NCAA) officers, and stars such as Martina Navratilova and Zina Garrison-Jackson. Curriculum available.

GAY, LESBIAN, AND BISEXUAL NETWORKS

More and more gay, lesbian, and bisexual professionals are joining networks that pertain to their fields and industries. Networking among people in the same field can break both personal isolation and career stagnation. Here are a few that exist in diverse fields.

Digital Queers
> 584 Castro Street #150
> San Francisco, CA 94114
> 415-252-6282
> *Network of gays, lesbians, and bisexuals in the computer industry.*

Federal GLOBE—Gay, Lesbian and Bisexual Government Employees
> P.O. Box 45237
> Washington, DC 20026-5237
> 202-986-1101
> *Network spanning 27 government agencies across the country.*

Gay and Lesbian Medical Association
> 273 Church Street
> San Francisco, CA 94114
> 415-255-4547
> *The national gay and lesbian doctors' association.*

Hi-Tech Gays
> P.O. Box 6777
> San Jose, CA 95150
> *Regional association of high-technology workers in the Silicon Valley.*

Lesbian and Gay Labor Network
> P.O. Box 1159
> Peter Stuyvesant Station
> New York, NY 10009
> *In 1990, published* Pride at Work, *a guide for unions and companies.*

National Lesbian and Gay Journalists Association
> 874 Gravenstein Highway, Suite 4
> Sebastopol, CA 95472
> 707-823-2193
> *Works for fair coverage of gay and lesbian issues in reporting and for fair treatment of gays and lesbians in the newsroom. Publishes* Alternatives *newsletter*

National Organization of Gay and Lesbian Scientists and Technical Professionals
> P.O. Box 91803
> Pasadena, CA 91109
> 818-791-7689
> *Nationwide association of professionals in the field of science.*

HELPFUL ORGANIZATIONS

Legal and Political Information

American Association of Sex Educators, Counselors, and Therapists
435 North Michigan Avenue, Suite 1717
Chicago, IL 60611-4067
312-644-0828
Provides education on sexuality for counselors, therapists, and teachers.

American Civil Liberties Union—Gay and Lesbian Rights Project
132 West 43rd Street
New York, NY 10036
212-944-9800 x545
Legal and political information on sexual orientation.

Gay and Lesbian Alliance Against Defamation (GLAAD)
150 W. 26th Street, Suite 503
New York, NY 10001
212-807-1700
National organization devoted to identifying and responding to public expressions of homophobia, particularly in the media, and to improving public understanding of the history and achievements of lesbians and gay men. Many chapters nationwide.

Human Rights Campaign Fund
1101 14th Street, NW, Suite 200
Washington, DC 20005
202-628-4160
Political organization committed to securing full civil rights for lesbians and gay men and responsible federal policies on AIDS. HRCF mobilizes grassroots support and lobbies, educates, and helps to elect legislators who support the goal of equality.

Lambda Legal Defense and Education Fund
666 Broadway, 12th Floor
New York, NY 10012
212-995-8585
Largest and oldest lesbian and gay legal organization, involved in fighting antigay and AIDS-related discrimination.

National Center for Lesbian Rights
870 Market Street, Suite 570
San Francisco, CA 94102
415-392-6257
The nation's only public service law firm dedicated to the legal concerns of lesbians. Provides no-fee legal services and litigates for law reform.

National Federation of Parents and Friends of Lesbians and Gays (P-FLAG)

1101 14th Street NW, Suite 1030
Washington, DC 20005
202-638-4200
Network of support groups for parents and friends of lesbians and gays. Offers library service of educational resource materials. Chapters exist throughout the country.

National Gay & Lesbian Task Force

2320 17th Street NW
Washington, DC 20009-2702
202-332-6483
One of the largest national lesbian and gay organizations, NGLTF focuses on lobbying, political organizing, and education on the topic of sexual orientation. NGLTF sponsors an annual conference on workplace issues, Out and Equal, *held in a different U.S. city each year. In addition, NGLTF has several pamphlets available on workplace issues.*

People for the American Way

2000 M Street NW, Suite 400
Washington, DC 20036
202-467-4999
Monitors antigay politics and provides resources and technical assistance.

Our Local Legal and Political Information Resources

_____

_____

_____

_____

_____

_____

_____

_____

_____

_____

_____

_____

_____

_____

_____

_____

_____

_____

_____

Other Helpful Organizations

Asian Pacifica Lesbian Network

P.O. Box 2594
Daly City, CA 94017
Largest national network of Asian Pacific lesbians.

Association of Lesbian and Gay Psychologists

2336 Market Street, No. 8
San Francisco, CA 94114
National network of psychologists.

National Latino/a Lesbian and Gay Organization (LLEGO)

703 G Street SE
Washington, DC 20003
202-544-0092
Network linking primarily gay and lesbian Latino/a organizations, AIDS service providers, and individuals.

Hetrick-Martin Institute, Inc.

2 Astor Place, 3rd Floor
New York, NY 10003
212-674-2400
Social service agency for lesbian and gay youth. Includes the Harvey Milk High School.

Project 10

Fairfax High School
7850 Melrose
Los Angeles, CA 90046
213-655-9202
Los Angeles Unified School District's counseling and support program for lesbian, gay, and bisexual students.

Senior Action in a Gay Environment (SAGE)

305 7th Avenue, 16th Floor
New York, NY 10001
212-741-2247
Multiservice program serving seniors in the lesbian and gay community. Intergenerational in its membership and volunteers. SAGE provides social services, socialization, education, and advocacy and offers the only AIDS program for seniors in the country.

RELIGIOUS ORGANIZATIONS

Affirmation/Mormons
Box 46022
Los Angeles, CA 90046
213-255-7251

Affirmation/United Methodists
Box 1021
Evanston, IL 60204
708-475-0499

American Baptists Concerned
872 Erie Street
Oakland, CA 94610
510-465-8652

Axios—Eastern and Orthodox Christian Gay Men and Women
P.O. Box 990, Village Station
New York, NY 10014
212-989-6211

Brethren/Mennonite Council for Lesbian and Gay Concerns
Box 6300
Minneapolis, MN 55406-0300
612-870-1501

Buddhist Association of the Gay and Lesbian Community
c/o Box 1974
Bloomfield, NJ 07003

Dignity/USA (Lesbian and Gay Catholics)
1500 Massachusetts Avenue NW, Suite 11
Washington, DC 20005
202-861-0017

Evangelicals Concerned
c/o Dr. Ralph Blair
311 East 72nd Street, Suite 1-G
New York, NY 10021
212-517-3171

Friends for Lesbian/Gay Concerns (Quakers)
Box 222
Sumneytown, PA 18084
215-234-8424

Integrity (Lesbian and Gay Episcopalians)
P.O. Box 19561
Washington, DC 20036-0561
718-720-3054

Lutherans Concerned
Box 1046, Ft. Dearborn Station
Chicago, IL 60610-0461

Metropolitan Community Churches, Universal Fellowship (Christian)
5300 Santa Monica Boulevard, Suite 304
Los Angeles, CA 90029
213-464-5100

National Gay Pentecostal Alliance
Box 1391
Schenectady, NY 12301-1391
518-372-6001

Presbyterians for Lesbian/Gay Concerns
Box 38
New Brunswick, NJ 08903-0038

Seventh-Day Adventist Kinship International
P.O. Box
Laguna Miguel, CA 92607
714-248-1299

Unitarian Universalist Office for Lesbian/Gay Concerns
25 Beacon Street
Boston, MA 02108
617-742-2100

World Congress of Gay and Lesbian Jewish Organizations
Box 18961
Washington, DC 20036

AIDS-RELATED ORGANIZATIONS

ACT UP (AIDS Coalition to Unleash Power)
New York Chapter:
135 W. 29th Street, 10th Floor
New York, NY 10001
212-564-2437
Diverse, nonpartisan group of individuals committed to direct action to end the AIDS crisis. Meets with government officials and holds demonstrations. Chapters exist in numerous cities worldwide.

AIDS Project Los Angeles (APLA)
1313 North Vine Street
Los Angeles, CA 90028
213-993-1600
Nonprofit, community-based organization dedicated to improving the quality of lives of people affected by HIV and AIDS through direct service provision, education, and public policy programs.

American Foundation for AIDS Research (AmFAR)
733 3rd Avenue, 12th Floor
New York, NY 10017
212-682-7440
Nation's leading private sector funding organization dedicated to AIDS research, education, and public policy.

Gay Asian Pacific Alliance's Community HIV Project
1841 Market Street
San Francisco, CA 94103
415-575-3939
Provider of prevention, education, and support services to Asian and Pacific Islander gay and bisexual men.

Gay Men's Health Crisis (GMHC)
129 West 20th Street
New York, NY 10011
212-807-6664
Largest AIDS service organization and a national model for organizations caring for people with AIDS, educating the public about the epidemic, and advocating for fair, effective AIDS policy.

Minority AIDS Project—LA

5149 West Jefferson Boulevard
Los Angeles, CA 90016
213-936-4949
First community-based AIDS organization established and managed by people of color in the United States to increase education and coordinate access to health services for the underserved people of color communities as well as people living with HIV and AIDS.

Minority Task Force on AIDS—NYC

505 8th Avenue, 16th Floor
New York, NY 10018
212-563-8340
Private community-based organization providing education and direct support services for people infected and affected by the HIV and AIDS epidemic.

Mobilization Against AIDS

584 B Castro Street
San Francisco, CA 94114
415-863-4676
Health advocacy group focused on securing early treatment for people with HIV. Coordinator of annual International AIDS Candlelight Memorials.

NAMES Project (AIDS Memorial Quilt)

310 Townsend Street, Suite 310
San Francisco, CA 94107
415-882-5500
AIDS memorial taking the shape of a huge quilt made of individual 3' x 6' panels, each representing an individual who has died of AIDS.

National Association of People With AIDS

1413 K Street NW
Washington, DC 20005
202-898-0414
Assistance to people with AIDS nationwide, speakers bureau, and national computer bulletin board.

National Minority AIDS Council

300-I Street NE, Suite 400
Washington, DC 20002
202-544-1076
Provider of HIV education and advocacy for and about community-based organizations that serve various ethnic and cultural populations.

National Native American AIDS Prevention Center (NNAAPC)
> 2100 Lakeshore Avenue, Suite A
> Oakland, CA 94606
> 510-444-2051
> *Training, technical assistance, and information services to Native American communities on HIV prevention.*

San Francisco AIDS Foundation
> 25 Van Ness Avenue, Suite 660
> San Francisco, CA 94102
> 415-864-5855
> *Support services to people with AIDS, multicultural education about AIDS, and public policy and media-related work.*

Our Local AIDS-Related Resources

_____

_____

_____

_____

_____

_____

_____

_____

_____

_____

_____

DOMESTIC PARTNER BENEFITS RESOURCES

National Gay & Lesbian Task Force—Workplace Project
2320 17th Street NW
Washington, DC 20009
202-332-6483 x3361
Domestic Partner Organizing Manual *and other publications available.*

Richard Jennings
Hollywood Supports
8455 Beverly Boulevard, Suite 305
Los Angeles, CA 90048
213-655-7705
Established domestic partner benefits in the entertainment industry.

LEAGUE (Lesbian and Gay United Employees of the Walt Disney Company)
500 S. Buena Vista Street
Burbank, CA 91521-5209
Created The ABC's of Domestic Partner Benefits *for Disney.*

Andrew Sherman, Vice President
The Segal Company
116 Huntington Avenue
Boston, MA 02116-5712
617-424-7337
Has aided other companies in establishing domestic partners benefits programs.

Stanford University Report on Domestic Partner Benefits
College and University Personnel Association
1233 20th Street NW, Suite 301
Washington, DC 20036-1250
202-429-0311 x395
The most comprehensive report (70 pages) on establishing a benefits plan.

The Gay/Lesbian/Bisexual Corporate Letter
104 East 31st Street, Suite 4B
New York, NY 10016-6816
212-447-7328
Newsletter on workplace issues and news.

LANDMARK GAY AND LESBIAN EVENTS

1994 2.1 million visit New York City to celebrate 25th anniversary of 1969 Stonewall Riots.

1990 Hate Crimes Statistics Act, first federal law to include "sexual orientation."

1988 National Education Association supports school counseling on sexual orientation.

1986 Supreme Court upholds right of states to criminalize sexual relations.

1982 Wisconsin prohibits discrimination against lesbians and gays.

1979 200,000 attend first Gay Rights March on Washington.

1978 California defeats issue to expel lesbians and gay school workers and gay rights supporters.

1973-74 Homosexuality removed from list of mental disorders.

1971 National Organization of Women acknowledges oppression of lesbians.

1968 Metropolitan Community Church founded by lesbian and gay Christians in Los Angeles.

1967 First gay protest march in U.S. protests Los Angeles Police Department arrests.

1960 Model Penal Code urges decriminalization of same-sex sexual acts.

1955 First lesbian organization, The Daughters of Bilitis, formed in San Francisco.

1951 Mattachine Society formed in Los Angeles (over 100 groups in Southern California by 1953).

1947 McCarthy purges thousands of homosexuals from federal jobs.

1924 Society for Human Rights, first formal U.S. gay movement group, forms in Chicago.

1992 President Clinton announces "don't ask, don't tell" policy for gays in the military.

1989 Massachusetts prohibits discrimination against lesbians and gay men.

1987 500,000 at second March on Washington for Lesbian and Gay Rights.

1985 First mention of AIDS by President Reagan four years after epidemic begins.

1981 First reference to AIDS as "gay disease" in medical journals.

1978 Assassination of Supervisor Harvey Milk and San Francisco Mayor George Moscone.

1977 Harvey Milk first openly gay person elected to public office.

1971 Connecticut, Colorado, and Oregon repeal sodomy laws.

1969 Stonewall Riots in New York for rights to gather in public start the modern lesbian and gay liberation movement.

1967-68 Support groups emerge on college campuses such as Columbia and New York University.

1961 Illinois is first state to decriminalize private homosexual acts of consenting adults.

1958 First U.S. Supreme Court win for lesbians and gays—*One* may be mailed.

1954 *One,* the first magazine for lesbians and gays published in Los Angeles.

1948 Kinsey Report startles Americans with number of men engaged in same-sex acts.

1945 Many lesbian and gay World War II veterans settle urban lesbian and gay communities.

1890s to 1920s Establishment of lesbian and gay social institutions in major U.S. cities.

MY PERSONAL LANDMARKS

8-15-96   Today, I completed a book on sexual orientation. I got a lot of questions answered, and I have a lot of ideas about how to bring this topic to my organization.

Date

ABOUT THE AUTHORS

Amy J. Zuckerman is a trainer, consultant, and author on diversity issues, with an emphasis on sexual orientation. She is also General Manager at George Simons International, a consulting firm specializing in cross-cultural and gender diversity management. She has contributed to and edited new editions of *Working Together: Succeeding in a Multicultural Organization* and the needs assessment anthology *The Questions of Diversity*. She has also developed customized versions of the training instrument *DIVERSOPHY™ : Understanding the Human Race* on sexual orientation, gender communication, sexual harassment, and various international business issues. She is a lesbian who frequently writes on the topic of sexual orientation in the workplace.

George F. Simons is a management consultant and trainer who specializes in gender and cultural diversity issues in the workplace. With over thirty years' experience helping people to understand, accept, and manage their differences creatively and productively, he is in demand worldwide as a speaker, adviser, and seminar leader. He is the leading designer of the *DIVERSOPHY™* game, author of *Transcultural Leadership* (with Carmen Vázquez and Philip Harris), and a coeditor of *The Questions of Diversity*. In the Crisp Videobook series, he has developed two best sellers: *Working Together: Succeeding in a Multicultural Organization,* now in its second edition, and *Men and Women: Partners at Work,* a collaboration with G. Deborah Weissman. He is heterosexual.

NOTES

NOTES

NOTES